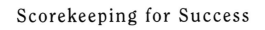

Scorekeeping for Success

Also by Charles A. Coonradt

Managing The Obvious
The Four Laws of Debt Free Prosperity
The Game of Work

SCOREKEEPING FOR SUCCESS

Charles A. Coonradt
with Lee Benson

PARK CITY, UTAH

The Game of Work, Inc.
1912 Sidewinder Drive Suite 201
Park City, Utah 84060
800-438-6074
email: game@gameofwork.com
www.gameofwork.com

First edition, 1998

Library of Congress Catalogue Number
97-95316
Coonradt, Charles A.
    Scorekeeping for success.
    Includes index.
ISBN 1-883004-05-5
Printed in the United States of America
10 9 8 7 6 5 4 3 2

To my partner forever, Carla, and my children, Christina, Kelly, Christopher, Cody, and Christian.

And to very special scorekeepers Rex Houze, who taught me that $200 more a month can build a fortune, and William E. Shea, who throughout his life encouraged me to build this business for the development of better managers and coaches everywhere.

ACKNOWLEDGEMENTS

My heartfelt thanks go out to the following people: To the open-minded and progressive chief executive officers of thousands of companies who have been receptive to these innovative yet well-founded principles of improving employee involvement and enthusiasm, and corporate profitability.

To Carla, my partner in life and business forever, without whom the experiences to create this work would not have happened and without whom the assemblying, editing and bringing to publication of this work would still be a mangled manuscript on the work room floor.

To Chuck Acklin,—a fulltime associate of THE GAME OF WORK since 1994, and a raving fan for a decade before,—for being my alter-ego and assisting in the structure and clarity of my creativity.

To Nancy Swenson, my keeper, who keeps me on time, at the right place, with the right folks, and with the right material to get the job done.

To Lee Benson, who was always available to fit into the seams of my schedule with tremendous professionalism, savvy examples, and unrelenting research to provide the parallels in sport to reinforce the key points of scorekeeping. Without Lee, this book would have been a list of 48 non-sentences of good ideas.

To Roger Romrell, a friend, a mentor, a true scorekeeper and a true winner, for his willingness to edit and help us maintain the appropriate international focus.

To Rick Williams, a very special implementer and associate of

THE GAME OF WORK, for his constant challenging and expanding of our concepts with our clients.

To Steve Smith of Utility Trailer, a great fan, friend, and practitioner of our concepts since the publication of THE GAME OF WORK. Thanks for your unique insights and willingness to be as educational on the chairlift up as you have been on the hill going down.

To the tens of thousands of GAME OF WORK participants who have dedicated their time, energy, and unique personal interpretations and experiences to translate my ideas into functional, delivering scorecards in hundreds of industries around the world. To this group, who came to be taught but who wound up teaching me, I am deeply indebted.

CONTENTS

INTRODUCTION

Why you should read this book

*It's what you learn
after you think
you know it all
that really matters.*

—JOHN WOODEN

Twenty years ago, I thought I knew it all.

I had just stumbled onto a workplace concept that would eventually become THE GAME OF WORK, and the response from the business community was, to say the least, gratifying. The principle idea behind THE GAME OF WORK is for companies, managers, and employees alike to treat work as if it were a game; to incorporate the motivational aspects of recreation, as well as the drive of organized sports, into the business arena so you can *work like you play.* From the start, the reception received by this simple, uncomplicated concept bordered on overwhelming.

The discovery had been preceded by a question. Why, I had asked myself, is it that people will pay for the privilege of working harder than they will work when they are paid? Why do people working in the frozen food industry, as an example, need to be paid premium wages and bonuses because they are required to work in the cold—yet those same people, when they are off work, will drive to a ski resort, pay fifty dollars for a day pass, and the only time they'll complain is if you make them go inside where it's warm?

Or, why is it that people will complain all day long if you make them work in a building where the temperature is 80 degrees, yet as soon as the shift ends they're on the tennis court or the golf course, where it's even hotter—and they'll play until the sun goes down?

Why do people pay for the privilege of working harder than they will work when they are paid?

The answer was as simple as the question: we are attracted to that which motivates us, that which identifies our goals, and that which gives us a clear indication of how we're progressing.

Those, of course, are the primary components and dynamics that are ever-present in the games we choose to play.

THE GAME OF WORK simply calls for the workplace to adopt similar measurements used when people play games. *Management by measurement* is what I called the concept two decades ago, proud of the alliteration, excited about the possibilities.

And it works! The thousands of companies, tens of thousands of managers, and millions of employees who have greatly increased their productivity and their workplace environment and morale by employing the principles of THE GAME OF WORK are living proof of that. We have offered our unique money-back guarantee—any company that doesn't feel it has realized a 100 percent return on its money four months after we implement the process is free to ask for a refund—across the United States and around the world. The feedback has been consistently positive. *Working like you play* doesn't cost, it pays off.

Beyond that, more than a hundred thousand copies of our

breakthrough book, THE GAME OF WORK, have been sold, with yearly sales averages continuing at a steady pace—unheard of results for an unknown author and regional publisher.

And yet, along with the overwhelmingly positive responses received by THE GAME OF WORK, and despite all the success stories and increased productivity, a common question persisted pertaining to measurement.

Exactly "what and how," people wanted to know, should they measure?

At first, I resisted these specific questions about measurement, clinging to my belief that once a system of management by measurement, or, as it is also known, TQM (Total Quality Management) was in place, the measuring would simply evolve and take care of itself. It would be a natural process. If the concept wasn't working as well at one place as another, it must be the fault of the individuals or the management involved, not the system. The traditional methods of measuring already in place simply had to be updated.

That's what I believed.

I was mistaken.

What I have come to realize is that "what and how" we measure requires a good deal of attention. Further, I have come to appreciate the fact that the traditional measuring done in companies—*the way we've always done it*—is not only not enough, but can be actually counterproductive.

Only when we successfully transform our measuring into something tangible, relevant, and meaningful do we allow management by measurement to really take off.

That transformation is called scorekeeping.

Scorekeeping, not mere measurement, is the key.

Scorekeeping is what makes THE GAME OF WORK work.

Scorekeeping is why ten people with a volleyball and a net at the company picnic can achieve teamwork and goal direction and become a well-managed work team in a matter of minutes; whereas mere measurement is why the same ten people can totally and completely fail to achieve that kind of harmony on the job and, worse, spend all day protecting their turf.

This book is about the success that can be realized by observing the principles of sound scorekeeping. It contains a compilation of material that represents the culmination of nearly two decades of research, experimentation, and observation of what goes into and makes up successful scorekeeping. It chronicles twenty years of creating scorecards in places they have never been before, in industries where no one thought they could be implemented. It is twenty years worth of learning what scorekeeping can do, and the startling, often revolutionary, results.

There are no strings attached. This powerful concept is universally applicable. Available to one and all. Once the strategies of successful scorekeeping are understood and implemented, they can increase productivity and profitability no matter what the size of your business, no matter what your management style, no matter how grandiose or how modest your goals.

I am confident that in the collection of examples and experiences that follow, one or more will apply to your particular circumstances and help you in your own particular enterprise.

- Chapters 1 through 5 explore the powerful psychologies and philosophies of scorekeeping. Why it is valuable. Why it works. Why it can work for you.

- Chapters 6 through 19 identify the major concepts of scorekeeping that, when added together, establish a firm foundation for understanding and setting up effective scorecards.

- Chapters 20 through 24 outline exactly HOW to set up your own scorekeeping systems.

- I conclude in chapter 26 by sharing a personal story of "keeping score" that worked for me.

As with our landmark publication, THE GAME OF WORK, you'll find that the contents are sprinkled liberally with sports stories and examples. I collaborated with a sports writer to research some of the topics and help with the writing. My business isn't to convert sports fans or in any way make this a sports book, but I've found no better source than the world of games for parallels we can follow so we can indeed "work like we play."

What you're about to read is what we've learned at THE GAME OF WORK since I thought I knew it all.

Chuck Coonradt
THE GAME OF WORK
Park City, Utah

The Power of
Scorekeeping

WHY KEEP SCORE

*When you want to know
if you're winning or losing,
look at the scoreboard.*

It is my premise that every day, we all come to work with this question in mind:

How Do I Win?

Now that might be phrased, and disguised, in a variety of ways. How do I get by? How do I survive? How do I keep from being fired? How do I please my boss? How do I make it to the end of the day?

But at the bottom of it all, we all want to be able to answer the same fundamental question:

How do I win?

If the answer is clear, great. But if that question can't be answered satisfactorily, then we've got trouble.

If we're confused about how to win, the mind is going to conclude:

Must be no way to win.

And that's a problem, because once we say to ourselves, *No way to win*, the statement that naturally follows is:

Why try?

Why try when I can't win?

And *Why try?* is going to naturally be followed by:

Might as well quit.

Many workers—way too many from what I've seen—pass quickly through the *Why try?* and *Might as well quit* phases. At which point they hit the brakes hard and come to a dead standstill. They've had it. They're through. Finished. Disconnected.

Now if they quit and leave, that's not good, because that creates turnover. But at least it gives the company a chance to replace them with someone else and try again.

It's when they quit and *stay* that we get a virus in the workplace, and low morale, and contamination that spreads and spreads, with the capacity to cripple companies large and small.

This doesn't happen only once in a while.

I was talking to a CEO of a large company and, looking for a head count, I asked him, "How many people do you have working here?"

"Just over half," he answered, "near as I can tell."

Then I asked, "What's your biggest problem?"

"Unannounced early retirement," he said.

At many companies, their most sizeable problem, by far, is getting their workers to work while they're at work; to buy into what they're doing and reflect that purchase by behavior that's efficient, productive, and resourceful.

The reason this is such a widespread, sometimes debilitating, problem is simply because most American workers Don't ... Know ... How ... To ... Win.

They ask themselves that question and they come up blank.

They honestly don't know.

They don't know what it takes to win. They're confused. They don't know how to score points, let alone win the game. Sometimes they're not even sure where the playing field is, let alone whether it's level. Other times the playing field moves. One day they're asked to do one thing, one day another. Much of their work energy is spent trying to decide which supervisor to please. Going to work becomes a different kind of game—a guessing game.

It's often just as murky at the top. Management can also become paralyzed. They may not know how to win, or if their return on investment reflects winning or losing. Too many supervisors and managers, lacking the answers to the "win" question, aren't any more sure of what's expected of them than the people they're managing. They don't know how to win either, and the only thing management is sure of is that the expectations tend to change from day to day. One day it's: "Serve the customer whatever it takes." The next day: "Increase return on investment." Followed by: "Quality is the only thing that counts."

Confusion never inspired anyone. Think about it. What happens if we're confused in the way we parent? What if we tell our kids different things on different days? One day it's: "I want straight A's." The next day it's: "I want you to be popular." The next it's: "I want you to follow strict standards." And the next it's: "I want you to excel in sports or band or drama."

Once a kid gets too many conflicting messages, the domino process inevitably begins. He or she is going to conclude: *No way to win ... Why try? ... Might as well quit.* Once that domino thought process is underway, all of our parenting, however well-intentioned, isn't going to count for very much, and it certainly isn't going to yield positive results. If we don't make our expectations clear and allow children's input and goals to effect those expectations, and then keep them constant, the best we can hope for is controlled confusion.

If we don't allow our kids to know how they can win, we're going to have rebellion on our hands. It might be active rebellion, it might be passive, it might not even be detectable on the surface, but the one thing we can count on is that it will be there.

It's the same in the business world. Because of unclear and conflicting expectations, confusion and rebellion rule.

Have you noticed how some companies wake up and "suddenly" find themselves with all this deadweight, with all these programs that are deemed passé, with all these people they don't need? In one well-publicized case a few years ago, IBM one day, out of the blue, announced it was laying off some 70,000 people. Now how in the world does IBM all of a sudden wake up one morning with 70,000 excess employees? How does that happen? You find yourself wondering, "What did all these people do yesterday?" and "Who's going to do tomorrow what they did yesterday?"

But in reality, you just know that these layoffs were a long time in coming. In business, especially, there's no such thing as "all of a sudden." There is nothing overnight about layoffs. They are simply the end result of a way of doing business that is scattered, conflicting, and confused. When the chaos reached a climax at IBM, that's when the "suddenly" came in and, just like that, it was discovered that the jobs of 70,000 people were immediately expendable.

The message emerging from such a disaster is that the company wasn't getting the job done when it came to telling its employees, and itself, how to win. Too many people were coming to work without an answer or a goal or an objective. They had no way to know.

That is why we keep score.

So we can know.

Each of us.

Every day.

How to win.

Effective scorekeeping provides the reckoning and a system for feedback so that everyone—from the CEO down to the last person on the last shift of the day—can personally know how to win. Beyond that, they can also know how to accurately and consistently gauge just how they're doing along the way.

Once we establish a scorekeeping system that allows everyone to clearly tell when they're winning, and when they're not; once we've

> **Because of unclear and conflicting expectations, confusion and rebellion rule.**

eliminated that gray, foggy area that gives us a place to hide, the more we're going to thrive, and succeed, in the long run.

"Every Day Everyone Needs to Know How to Win at Their Job!"

The fundamental principle to keep in mind is, that everyone, from the Chairman of the Board down the line, wants to know—

"How do I win?"

If we do not answer that question, at an individual level on a daily basis, we risk their default thought—

"There is no way to win here!"

If that thought creeps in, the next thought in the domino process is—

"Why should I try?"

That questioning thought will lead to the inescapable conclusion—

"I quit!"

Now the worker has a choice. He can quit and leave and create a vacancy. Or, he can quit and stay. When he quits and stays, he creates a virus of disconnecting and disenchantment, then recruits others to his way of thinking. The results are people who simply show up and work without contributing. Workers and managers (coaches) have too great an impact on our business for us to risk the consequences of not letting them know, specifically and frequently the answer to this question—

"How do I win, here, today, with you, Coach?"

We can eliminate the virus, improve performance, and reduce turnover at the coaches level because—

"How workers feel about their company is primarily effected by how they feel about their Coach!"

Identifying the Problem

The problem in most businesses is that scorekeeping just doesn't get much thought. Even when some kind of score is kept, it's often the wrong score or it's done with an outdated system.

Remember when I used the example of employees at the company picnic being able to band together in a matter of minutes on the volleyball court, harmoniously pursuing a similar goal, yet those same people can work side by side in the workplace for years and never come close to that kind of unity? Well, what's the difference? The difference is that the volleyball game not only has a clearly defined goal—to be the first to get to 21 points—it also has a clearly defined way of identifying which team is winning.

How do you win in volleyball? How do you score points? With a team that has order and focus, that's how. As a result, teams get quickly organized. Team members cover the court, each person responsible for his or her own area. One person serves, others pass, others set, still others spike. Everyone becomes involved in the cause—the winning cause—of getting the ball over the net and scoring points.

After every point, it's easy to determine whether your team is winning or losing. Just check the score. If you're ahead, great. If you're behind, you're going to see the need to do some adjusting. Somebody might reorganize the rotation, alternating the shorter team members with the taller ones. Somebody else might give a tip to a less experienced player. It might be the accountant telling the vice president of finance how to spike the ball, but that's OK, because everybody knows what you're trying to do. You're trying to win.

Now contrast this scene with what happens when these co-workers show up the next morning at the office. They report to their usual posts. They keep interaction to a bare minimum. They concentrate on individual activity, on protecting their "own turf." The contrast from this to the cohesiveness at the volleyball court the day before is glaring. Where there was harmony, now there's dissonance. Where there was a commonality of a goal, now there's fragmentation. These people are still very much a team, but, back in the office they are a dysfunctional one. They have little unity. They're confused as to just what it is they are trying to accomplish, and, worst of all, there is little or no agreement as to what the score is. The only common cause is a lost one. And deep down everyone knows it. The goal isn't winning any more, it's surviving.

The only ways to "keep score" are the vague, obscure, and traditional methods—largely unspoken—that have been in place longer than anyone can remember. Maybe it's whether the boss knows you by name. Maybe it's what kind of view you have out your office window, or who got which hand-me-down computer. Maybe it's if you still have the same accounts. Maybe it's based on the last employee evaluations, which took place nine months ago. Whatever it is, it's not all that forthcoming and it varies from team member to team member.

Months and years go by, and nothing much ever changes. Offices become caves; company positions become so many island kingdoms, protected by well-placed mental moats; and the "team" blindly weaves its way from paycheck to paycheck, surviving but not thriving, constantly muttering "Why try?," "Might as well quit," and, in some cases, "I quit."

Company positions become so many island kingdoms, protected by well-placed mental moats.

Would a game such as volleyball ever tolerate such chaos and confusion? Would it allow the score to be a mere murky afterthought, ignored and practically disregarded?

Why should we tolerate chaos and confusion in the workplace? Why not implement what works on the volleyball court at the office?

In games, knowing the score, and computing it the best way possible, is paramount. Sports associations are constantly tinkering with the way their game is played and scored. They take care to ensure that the scorekeeping is conducive to fair play and thus able to maximize the competitive experience. Rule books are concise, clear, well conceived, and constantly updated for the good of the game.

For example, in basketball both the NCAA and the NBA are constantly looking at and tinkering with the distance from which a three-point goal is scored, and in golf, the United States Golf Association sent tremors through the golf equipment manufacturers with the mere threat that oversized drivers might not be acceptable. But in both instances, once deliberations were complete, consistency and clear expectations returned to the game.

Games identify how we need to pull together and work toward a goal; but most importantly, games let us know "How We Can Win." They leave no mystery about what is required to succeed. We need to implement the scorekeeping that works so well in our games into the workplace, and effectively eliminate the mystery about what is required to succeed there as well.

2

MEASUREMENT ISN'T SCOREKEEPING

Keeping score is more
than merely keeping track.

Ever have that nagging feeling that something's just not right? Yet you just don't know what?

Why is it that some of our GAME OF WORK clients enjoyed results that were instantaneous and sensational, while other clients experienced a much more modest return in productivity and employee enthusiasm?

What was the difference? Why didn't measurement by management work equally well across the board?

The concept of "working like you play" was a good one. But, still, the results were uneven. That couldn't be denied. Over time it became more and more obvious that something was missing. What was it?

It turned out to be right in front of our eyes.

This is what we discovered. The difference between those companies where THE GAME OF WORK took off like a rocket and those companies where it didn't was in WHAT and HOW they measured.

Those clients who measured the areas that directly and positively affected productivity, and who measured them in a timely fashion, enjoyed results that went well beyond their expectations. Those clients who failed to identify and measure the "right" areas, and who failed to be timely about it, enjoyed results somewhat less than spectacular.

It took time for us to realize that mere measurement is not scorekeeping.

We, as consultants, didn't see this at first because we weren't monitoring the emotion or human reaction, we were only monitoring the results. The measurements that were taking place were essentially reactive instead of proactive. We had not yet discovered the inherent differences between measurement and true scorekeeping.

When one of our manufacturing distribution clients insisted on measuring "less errors" in their delivery system and continued to make a big deal out of the errors when they occurred, they saw little improvement. When several of our clients used an accident/ frequency rate that was unclear to the players they got no improvement in performance.

We had not provided rules dealing with how to measure. Instead of making sure the measurement a client already had in place was capable of accurately telling and showing those involved exactly what was happening and how they could win, we simply allowed the measurement to take care of itself.

We had assumed measurement and scorekeeping were synonyms. But we came to realize those two words can have completely opposite meanings. The terms are not interchangeable.

Just because you have a measurement system in place doesn't mean you have a scorekeeping system in place.

Positive and Negative

The major difference between scorekeeping and measurement is that scorekeeping, by nature, is a positive process while measurement, by nature, is a negative process.

Scorekeeping identifies winners, not losers. Measurement, on the other hand, all too often points out only what's wrong, what's lacking, what's out-of-step. Measurement identifies losers, not winners.

> **The major difference between scorekeeping and measurement is that scorekeeping by nature is a positive process, while measurement by nature is a negative one.**

We tend to be a "measuring" society, and that doesn't always work to our advantage. Indeed, our penchant for "mere measuring" is responsible for much of the negative baggage we carry around. From our first steps or first words it begins. A child who walks at nine months is presumed to be more advanced or brighter than a child who walks at 11 months, although I know of no research that verifies that early walkers or early talkers, for that matter, enjoy a more fruitful, productive, or beneficial life. Yet, it is still an element of our society that urges such comparisons.

In our earliest rating systems in elementary school we get measured, and far too often, far too many of us just don't "measure up." We're too short, too fat, too average, too small, too thin, and so on. We go to the amusement park and find out we're not as tall as the sign so we can't ride the roller coaster.

As we walk through life we get bombarded by negative measurements.

Try this experiment on ten of your closest friends: ask them to describe themselves and see what you get. Chances are you'll get descriptions such as: "I'm too fat, too tall, too heavy, too bald ... too *something*." Ninety percent of people will answer with responses that are negative in nature, that indicate they know they are lacking in this area or that, that they don't feel like they *measure up*.

In many businesses, it's the same thing. Much of the measurement in the workplace accentuates the negative. Think about it. What do we typically measure? We measure errors. We measure overs and shorts. We measure what's out of stock. We measure mistakes. We even go so far as to measure safety by the number of accidents we've had in the past year.

The majority of workplace measurements track the errors, the mistakes, the foul-ups, the accidents, the short falls, the "whoopses." In retailing, what we really want is to be in-stock and the measurement tracks out-of-stock. Airlines want to be on time and they measure late arrivals. Banks want to make sure that their tellers are to-the-penny accurate. But teller accuracy is based on number of errors. Verify this sometime by going into your bank— that's the building behind the ATM machine—and asking the manager for the name of his or her most accurate teller.

The average bank manager will get this glazed look on his or her face and not be able to speak. They won't have a clue who is the bank's most accurate teller.

But change the request and ask for his or her most *inaccurate* teller, and you'll see an immediate change in facial expression. The manager will know instantly who makes the most mistakes. Why does the manager know? Because mistakes are what the bank measures.

Now think for a minute about the games we play. In our games, in our leisure-time recreation, what do we count? We count what is good, don't we? that which is positive. We may have missed shots, or even an occasional interception, but the enthusiasm in sport comes from achieving the positive results, not achieving fewer negatives.

We keep track of the hits, the goals, the touchdowns, the strokes, the service aces. When we're bowling we count the strikes. When we aim at a target, we "score" when we hit it, not when we miss.

We count the good instead of the bad in the games we play; the positive instead of the negative.

In a nutshell, that's the dichotomy between games and business, and the dichotomy between measurement and scorekeeping.

We don't say to a hockey player like Wayne Gretzky, "We'd like you to reduce the number of times you miss the net when you shoot." We just ask him to keep scoring goals. We don't ask Tiger Woods to count up his missed putts. We count his makes. We accentuate the positive. We keep score on what's good. Because that's what we want more of.

From our first experiences playing games, we understand how valuable it is to celebrate what's valuable. We count the number of repetitions when we skip the rope, the number of jacks we pick up, the number of base hits we get in Little League, the number of baskets we make. We keep score to win, not to lose. Batting averages in baseball tell the percentage of times we get a hit, not the percentage of times we don't. We keep track of home runs, not strikeouts—unless we're a pitcher, in which case we keep track of just the opposite. We track whatever's positive.

We celebrate the fact that Reggie Jackson hit 563 home runs to rank sixth on baseball's all-time list—not that he struck out 2,597 times. In basketball, we celebrate that Kareem Abdul-Jabbar scored 38,387 points during his NBA career, more than any player in history—not that he missed 12,470 shots.

Imagine what kind of career Reggie Jackson would have had if every time he'd come to the plate he'd have been worried about striking out, instead of just trying to hit a home run. What if they'd benched him because all the manager looked at and counted were his strikeouts? What if Kareem's performance had been judged according to missed shots, not makes? Would he have ever tried a low-percentage shot, one that had little chance of going in, but needed to be attempted because the shot clock was about to expire? Not if a miss would have been measured and then used against him.

If "not striking out" is what is being measured, if that's the score, then "not striking out" will become the goal—and few home runs will be hit. And in our businesses, "not striking out" is far too often the goal.

One of the emotional truths about people is that less negative does not automatically mean more positive.

Someone who focuses on "fewer errors, fewer errors, fewer errors," will inevitably do as little as possible in the areas where they can make errors. Instead of increased production, the result is decreased production—error-free, perhaps, but decreased just the same.

By keeping track of the negative, measurement can be debilitating to the point of freezing us right out of our potential.

But by tracking the positive, scorekeeping stimulates and prods us along to do more of the same. In contrast to measurement, scorekeeping motivates us.

A Big Difference

Measurement is what the nurse does when she measures how tall you are as a child, marks it at the doctor's office on a chart you'll never see again, and uses it to place you in a national percentile that lets you know you're not the tallest person in your age group in the country.

Scorekeeping is what your mother does when she periodically measures how tall you are as a child and makes a mark on the wall, charting your "growth" in a manner that is visible, encouraging, and stimulating.

The nurse's measurement will result in virtually nothing as far as your behavior is concerned, and can have the negative potential of generating a defeatist attitude based on the realization that a third, or half, or whatever, of the kids your age are taller than you are. It will NOT get you to drink your milk.

As for your mom's "scorekeeping," as you watch the marks she makes proceed progressively up the wall, those marks will motivate you; those marks WILL get you to drink your milk.

Similarly in business, a measurement system that charts manufacturing product loss, or retail out-of-stocks, or sales presentation failures, has all of that same measurement demotivation.

It's in organization where you're allowed to track the safe intervals of work between accidents, and celebrate improvements in your customer service percentages, that everyone involved is given the opportunity to experience that I-Can-Win feeling more often enjoyed on a golf course or a basketball court.

By tracking the positive, scorekeeping stimulates and prods us to do more of the same.

Quick Overview

Measurement / Scorekeeping

Measurement	Scorekeeping
Catches people doing it wrong	Reinforces behavior we want repeated
Is externally imposed	Is chosen by player
Is presented after game	Is dynamic
Forces competition	Allows competition
Maximizes excuses	Maximizes celebration
Discourages ownership	Stimulates ownership
Causes unnatural inhibition	Is natural stimulation
Is too big to correct	Is frequent enough to fix

A UNIVERSAL
LANGUAGE

Scorekeeping enables trust.

The Dow Jones Averages illustrate the power and universality of scorekeeping.

Even though no one knows what the Dow Jones Averages are.

Now, "no one" might be taking it a bit far. But not by much. I've gone around the world asking people, and mostly business people at that, to explain the Dow Jones Averages and usually what I get in response is a lot of throat-clearing, wild guesses, and blank stares. Very few people know just what the Dow Jones Averages are, and yet, in a very real sense, they drive the stock market climate not just in the United States but in exchanges from Paris to Hong Kong and everywhere in between. There may, in fact, be no greater influence on the world's economy.

When the "Dow" goes up, people cheer; when it goes down, people worry.

Because the Dow keeps score.

It is an accepted scoreboard that communicates how the New York stock market is doing. Around the world, the Dow's ability to act as an economic barometer is readily accepted—even though when we hear that the Dow has just "topped" 7,000 or 8,000, or probably even 10,000 before long, most of us don't have a clue exactly what that means.

All we know is that it is *meaningful*.

Why is this? Why have we so empowered the Dow?

The answer, I believe, is because of how much we all want to know what the score is. And the Dow tells us.

The story of how the Dow came to be is a story of the order and security that results when scorekeeping is established in a place it did not previously exist.

The origins of the Dow date back to the early days of the American stock market, when there was no real scoreboard, or scorekeeping system, in place on Wall Street.

In 1882, Charles Henry Dow and Edward David Jones started a

newsletter on Wall Street that they produced in their offices at 15 Wall Street, next door to the New York Stock Exchange. The stock market was in a fledgling state in those days, struggling to secure a favorable reputation in the financial community. Bonds, backed by hard assets, were the investment of choice. With innuendo and rumor customarily flying around Wall Street, stocks had an intangibleness that tended to scare off prudent investors.

It was the intent of Dow and Jones to bring a measure of stability to Wall Street, and make a profit for themselves in the bargain, by dispensing reliable, accurate and current news concerning the stock market.

Every weekday morning they would gather information, copy it by hand, and then dispatch messenger boys onto the streets to peddle their two-page news sheet—which they called the *Customer's Afternoon Letter*—to brokers and investors.

By 1889 the *Customer's Afternoon Letter* would have a catchier new name, one it uses to this day ... *The Wall Street Journal.*

Now inventing the *Wall Street Journal* might seem like plenty for one man's life's work, but the truth is, the *Wall Street Journal* might not be well into its second century as arguably the most successful newspaper in history, if Charles Henry Dow hadn't also been smart enough to come up with a way for Wall Street to keep score.

Which is where his "Averages" come in.

Dow knew he and Jones needed something compelling, something enticing, something *substantive*, to include in their afternoon newsletter so that investors would be compelled to buy it. What he came up with was a way, as the Dow Jones Company states in its own historical report, to *"make sense out of the confusion."*

"One hundred years ago, even people on Wall Street found it difficult to discern from the daily jumble of up-a-quarter and down-an-eighth whether stocks generally were rising, falling or treading water," the company account states. *"(So) Charles Dow devised his stock average. He began in 1884 by averaging the worth of 11 stocks, most of them railroads, which were the first great national corporations. He compared his average to placing sticks in the beach sand to determine, wave after successive wave, whether the tide was coming in or going out. If the average's peaks and troughs rose progressively higher, then a bull market prevailed; if the peaks and troughs dropped lower and lower, a bear market was on."*

What Dow Jones & Company sold Wall Street in the 1880's was a way to keep score. The *Wall Street Journal* began as a scoreboard.

"It seems simplistic nowadays with myriad market indicators," the Dow Jones historical account continues. *"But late in the Nineteenth Century it was like turning on a powerful new beacon that cut through the fog."*

The number of stocks in the "Dow" was increased from the original eleven to twelve in 1896, to twenty in 1916 and to thirty in 1928, where the number has stood ever since. "Industrial" was added to the name in 1896 when the railroad stocks were removed to help create what would become the "transportation" average, and yet another average designed to chart the rise and fall of utilities stocks—the "utilities" average—was also added. Thus the Dow's averages became plural, although the industrial average is the one that is commonly referred to when gauging the overall mood of the market.

In the beginning the computation was easy: Simply add up the prices of the stocks and divide by the number of stocks involved. That was the *average.* In 1928, however, editors at the *Wall Street Journal*—where an up-to-the-minute Dow is still published in every issue—began to calculate the average with a special devisor, computed to avoid distortions due to stock-splitting and/or stock substitutions. The result is what is now technically an "index" and not an "average." But facts are facts and tradition is tradition, and the Dow Jones *Average* it will always be.

I could run you through a mathematical explanation of how the *Journal* editors arrive at their ever-changing "devisor," but trust me when I tell you it's complicated.

For the purposes of our discussion, the computation doesn't matter, anyway. Just as it doesn't matter that almost no one knows exactly what makes up the Dow. What does matter is that the Dow works! It has been empowered now for well over a hundred years, showing no sign of wear and tear or letting up, because the people who watch its rises and falls have given it the thumbs-up. They accept it! They like it! Most importantly of all, they trust it!

It continues to be the way Wall Street keeps score.

As the Dow Jones & Company officially states, when the Dow came along it was "like turning on a powerful new beacon that cut through the fog." Those words paint a vivid picture of the power of keeping score. Scorekeeping cuts through the fog. It clarifies. By identifying and quantifying how we are doing, it creates motivation, energy, and drive where before there was none.

The Dow doesn't buoy investor confidence and make headlines on practically a daily basis in newspapers all around the world because people understand it, because many don't.

It buoys investor confidence and makes headlines because people around the world buy into it and readily accept it as a way of communicating the general health of the stock market and the economy. It is the language of choice.

The Dow is an excellent example of how once a fair method of keeping score is put in place and accepted, the results can be truly staggering. A New York Stock Market that now regularly handles over a *trillion dollars* worth of stocks is proof of that!

Everyone Speaks Scorekeeping

As the worldwide acceptance of the Dow helps attest, scorekeeping qualifies as a universal language, one that is capable of communicating across borders no matter how disparate the parties.

Think about it. If we needed to communicate with someone whose verbal language we couldn't understand and we had no idea where that person came from, wouldn't one of the best things we could do would be to show them sports equipment until we saw their eyes light up? Would we then have some common ground?

Roll out a volleyball, a basketball, a soccer ball, golf clubs, tennis rackets, boxing gloves, roll out any kind of sports equipment you can think of, and it isn't at all difficult to picture having a game in any of these activities with people from any diverse culture or background. We could take 22 kids from 22 different countries speaking 22 different languages, put them in position on a soccer field, and be able to orchestrate a totally goal-directed, highly enthusiastic, productive experience with *everyone* knowing what to do and what they're trying to accomplish. They would all know the goal, they would all know the score, and they would all know how to measure their activity against the score.

In the baseball major leagues, the Los Angeles Dodgers once had a pitching rotation that included players from the Dominican Republic, Mexico, Korea, Japan, and the United States. That's five nationalities and four languages on the same pitching staff! You'd think that would have created a major communication problem for the team, and particularly for the catcher, Mike Piazza, whose job was to work with each of these pitchers on a rotating basis. But when asked about all the different languages, Piazza said there were really no problems at all. Everybody knew the game of baseball. Everybody knew the various signs and signals, and, most importantly, everybody knew how to read the scoreboard. They all spoke *baseball*. The only problem was communicating *after*, not during the games, when it was hard for everybody to decide where to eat.

In the world of games, the record clearly shows time and again that people communicate just fine. At the Centennial Olympic Games in Atlanta, 197 nations, representing virtually every country on earth, speaking almost as many languages, came together and communicated side-by-side on the playing fields and courts without difficulty. It didn't matter what the venue was. Whether it was gymnastics, track & field, basketball, weightlifting, cycling, swimming, or any other sport, the competition proceeded as smoothly as if the competitors were from the same nation.

In so many areas of life, scorekeeping is the universal way that we assess value and effort. Scorekeeping is how we tell who's winning, who's losing, who's doing well, who's not doing well. Whether it's the Forbes 400 or the Pro Bowl, whether it's a Renoir masterpiece or a gymnast on the high bar, we know how to access it, how to understand it, how to appreciate it—because we know how to attach a score to it and how to interpret what that score means. The score can be stated in terms of money, as with a fine painting, or points, as with a gymnast, or by standings or averages or indexes or any of a number of manners of reckoning. There are all kinds of measurements we can use. But whatever the measurements, the score invariably comes through.

Scorekeeping is the universal way that we assess value and effort. Scorekeeping is how we tell who's winning.

Scorekeeping is second nature to us. Without having to stop and think about it, we routinely keep score in so many ways. We keep score relative to a resting pulse rate—we all know that 40 is better than 140. We keep score relative to cholesterol, to blood pressure, to grams of fat in our diet. Scorekeeping is how you get into medical school, it's how you get into Stanford. Scorekeeping decides who gets into the Boston Marathon; scorekeeping decides who wins the election.

Now, is there a difference between this universally accepted scorekeeping that we all routinely, without even thinking about it, accept and practice in our games and other areas of our lives, and what we commonly find practiced in American business? You bet there is. A big difference.

Whereas we intuitively use scorekeeping to help us know how to succeed, and win, in our games and in our personal life pursuits, in business we find that condition to be sorely lacking. In business, there is a resistance to implementing sound scorekeeping practices.

But that business mentality can change. The "universal language" of scorekeeping is fully capable of relating to what we do in our businesses as surely as it relates to what we do when we play. By keeping score at work like we do in our games, we can generate similarly satisfying results.

THE IMPORTANCE OF FEEDBACK

*Effort plus scorecard feedback
= Energy, Enjoyment, Enthusiasm.*

On an airline flight from New Orleans to Atlanta I found myself seated next to a gentleman, probably in his late thirties, who was poring over a stack of sales reports. Now sales reports by and large contain better fiction than any great American novel written. We know it's a game, know we have to do it, but we know if anyone believes it, well, they must have never been sales managers themselves.

This man was a regional sales manager with a well-known international package delivery service. Because of my curiosity in his business, I asked him about the sales reports. I said, "What do you do with them?"

"I send them to region," he said without much enthusiasm.

"What do they do with them?"

"Send them to corporate."

"Does anybody ever call you after they get them?"

"Nope," he said.

"Is there any chance anybody reads them?"

"I have no idea."

"Well why do you do it?" I asked, and, with a shrug of his shoulders, he responded, "Because they told me I have to."

My final question was this: "Do you suppose they'd miss it if you sent them late, or not at all?"

"I don't know," he said. Then he grinned and added, "But I've always wanted to try."

This man was a little less courageous than my good friend— I'll call him John—who worked as a sales manager for one of the Big Three auto companies. When I asked John for the secret of his success, he responded by saying, "I learned a long time ago never to send what they ask for the first time."

I said I didn't understand.

"The first time they ask for a report I don't send anything," he explained. "If they ask for it a second time, I get it finished and send it to them. That tells me they're going to actually look at it. But if I keep a report in the drawer for more than two business cycles and they don't ask for it again, I stop working on it and go on to something else. I figure, they're not going to look at it anyway, so what's the point?"

In organizations around the world, people fill out log sheets no one will ever check; people compile statistics and reports analysis and mail them to corporate and no one ever calls back.

No one likes their work to be unrecognized and unacknowledged.

Unfortunately, few of us have the courage of John, to tell them "No way," keep our sanity, and only work on what will get seen.

If it's important enough to do, it is important enough to keep score and give feedback on.

The astute business manager understands this: **if it's important enough to do, it's important enough to give feedback on. And if it's important enough to give feedback on, deliver that feedback in the most effective and valuable way available.**

Think of the power of those sales reports if, instead of disappearing into the black hole of "region" or "corporate," they are translated by thoughtful, insightful managers and turned into scorecards that will serve to inspire, motivate, and coordinate those sales managers, and their sales staffs, who created them in the first place!

Let Them Know

Someone once said that no one should be allowed to lead a company unless he or she has first house-trained a puppy.

I find great wisdom in that analogy. The principles at work in house-training a puppy run parallel to the primary principles needed when working with people.

One of the key rules for house-training a puppy is that you don't ever ask the puppy to do anything unless you then acknowledge that performance. Whatever it is. If the dog urinates on the paper you acknowledge that in a positive way, with a pat on the head, or a treat, or some other kind of reward. If the dog doesn't hit the paper, that needs to be acknowledged too, but in a way to make certain the puppy knows such behavior is not acceptable.

It is impossible *not* to provide feedback. The question is, will the feedback be consistent with the behavior we desire?

Too often in business, we make the request and then never respond to it. We ask the sales manager to send in his sales report and that's what the sales manager does—and then there is either no acknowledgement or the acknowledgement is very belated or incomplete. It might be good to note here that sending an e-mail acknowledgement of "Received" is *not* feedback. Webster defines feedback as "The return to the point of origin of evaluation or corrective information about an action or process." Most of the time, the report disappears into a black hole in a corner of an office somewhere at corporate headquarters. Like a puppy with no direction, the sales manager isn't quite sure what to do next.

Far better to not only send the sales manager feedback on the sales report, but to turn the sales report into an effective scorecard that allows the sales manager to participate in determining whether that feedback is going to be negative or positive.

This whole concept of assigning value to assignments by creating appropriate scorecards and then giving appropriate feedback carries with it tremendous power and potential. By giving everyone involved the valuable input of "knowing how to win," a total "win" situation is created for everyone involved.

This point was driven home simply, but dramatically, to me when THE GAME OF WORK got involved with a supermarket that was anxious to increase its productivity during the shopping day's slow times.

One area in the supermarket that experienced a real meltdown during the afternoons was the bakery, where, as you might guess, sales dropped off to practically nothing about mid-afternoon. To counter that, we set up a promotion that offered incentives. Free donuts. Every afternoon, announcements from the bakery would come across the loudspeakers offering a hot, fresh donut to anyone who would walk back to the bakery and get it. Since there is something especially seductive about the smell of freshly baked donuts, even at three o'clock in the afternoon, a lot of people would walk back to get their free donut and wind up buying a dozen more. Donut sales went up by an average of 40 to 50 dozen a day because of that promotion.

So far, so good. But upon further examination, we found that the key to making it all work was the bakery clerk who made the announcement. If she came across as enthusiastic and spirited, she would typically give away, and in turn sell, a lot of donuts. If she wasn't particularly energetic, however, the promotion fell flat. It all hinged on her and her presentation.

The store had a choice. It could merely hope its bakery clerk was energetic that day, or it could help ensure that the bakery clerk would be motivated to be energetic ... by creating a bakery clerk's scorecard.

In addition to the scorecards we'd set up that listed the store's overall goals, we helped set up an individual scorecard for the bakery clerk. She got her very own. It showed how often she did the announcement, how much she sold off the announcement, and so forth, with goals and bonuses tied into those goals. Every day, the bakery clerk would turn in her "score," and just as often, her coaches in the store's management would react with the appropriate response.

With that simple step of implementing a scorecard, and the appropriate feedback from management, a bakery clerk not making much more than minimum wage became a valuable part of the store's "team." The bakery clerk became an energetic, motivated employee. Her scorecards, and the interest taken in them by management, said to her that what she was asked to do was important, and because it was important to do, it was important enough to keep score on and to give feedback.

More to Come

In the chapters that follow, we'll look more closely at the relationship between management and workers, or, as we call them in THE GAME OF WORK, "coaches" and "players."

As we examine the importance of positive interaction between them, we will look at the necessary elements of feedback, ownership, buy-in, credibility, relevancy, goals, performance standards, and bonus compensation, all of which we've just introduced with something as simple, yet powerful, as the example of the bakery clerk.

The Power of
Scorekeeping

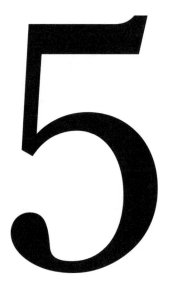

SCOREKEEPING
FIRST

*Set goals after, not before,
you know the score.*

Conventional corporate thinking says that when you wade into the murky area of productivity expectations, i.e. company goals, you begin with a set of corporate values.

From that, a mission statement is generated.

Next comes the establishment of a strategic plan.

And finally, a tactical "game plan" emerges, which is, of course, rolled out to the troops to deploy.

Usually what happens after all this managerial energy is expended in planning, setting direction, and establishing guidelines, someone in the back of the room will raise their hand and ask, "How do we know if we're getting there? If we're making any headway?" And somebody else will invariably respond, "We ought to have a way of measuring this. We should set some goals."

That's typically how corporate goals are set, goals that are an outgrowth of the expectations of management.

There's nothing wrong with that process.

Other than that it's completely backward.

What we generally find is that these well-meaning business goals founded solely on corporate expectations that have practically no basis in history are dismissed as either *incredible!* or *impossible!*, and often both, by the people who are given the responsibility to achieve them.

We've all seen it happen. The goals come down from management, the work force takes one look at them and gasps! After throwing their hands in the air, they then sound the well-known worker's lament: "How did you come up with this?!"

What follows next is motivational disconnect, which is where a majority of the people on the team will now spend considerably more time working on their rationalizations for not accomplishing the goals than they will in working at figuring out how the goals might actually get accomplished.

These kinds of business goals are generated by hopes and

dreams instead of by rational reality. Their existence is proof of the axiom that: **Nothing is impossible to those who are not responsible for achieving it.**

Nothing is impossible for those who are not responsible for achieving it.

A far better approach to goal-setting—and we have found verification for this with client after client—is to first begin scorekeeping on the various key indicators and results-to-resources ratios (how much is being accomplished with the resources available), and THEN establish goals. Do the homework and research before deciding what is reasonable to try to achieve.

It is noble to have high goals. It is impressive when we say we want to dominate the marketplace. It's easy to say that we should have a 75 percent market share, or some other astronomical number. Any corporate management returning from a high-level, high-priced retreat can sound lofty and far-thinking by boldly announcing such a goal. But it will make far greater sense to the people involved in the production effort to first go out and build some historical perspective on what the market share is in fact today.

It is infinitely more realistic and reasonable to establish scorecards that show what our current level of quality is, and then set goals based on realistic possibilities that can be easily measured by the method of scorekeeping we've put into place. It's scorekeeping that will ensure our goals will be met, not just set.

Breaking It Down

To help illustrate this concept of the importance of putting scorekeeping before goalsetting, and to emphasize how it works in games, let's turn to golf, a sport integrally tied to scorecards.

Let's say my average score for 18 holes is 90 strokes. If I want to set a goal for my golf game, which would be to shoot lower scores, I could take the corporate approach, which would be to retire to a luxury hotel-spa for a nice weekend retreat and there set my goal. While enjoying my surroundings, I'll think about what kind of golfer I'd like to be, and by the end of my retreat I will emerge with my goals for the coming year, which might be to lower that average to 80.

But let's face it, no matter how much I think about it and no matter how much I might want it, improving from 90 to 80 would be just a hopeful expectation, a dream based on nothing more than a desire to do a lot better this year than last.

It would be difficult for me to buy into a belief that I could indeed lower my 18-hole score by an average of 10 shots per round just because I thought long and hard about it and decided that's what I wanted to do. In my corporate mode, that might be what I'd like to achieve; but in my worker's mode, I'm going to think "this is impossible," because I have no idea how I'm going to pull it off.

A far better approach would be to first break down my golf scores from the past year and identify where I am losing most of my strokes to par (for our purposes here, let's assume par to be the standard 72 strokes per 18-hole round).

If I can break down my average rounds of 90 enough to let me see where I'm having my most trouble, then I can begin to set goals based on realistic expectations for improvement in those areas.

Let's say that I start out by taking all the par 5's I've played and putting them on one of my new "expanded" scorecards, and then I do the same with the par 4's and the par 3's. Now I can begin to better see just where I'm wasting my strokes. If my average on the par 3's is, say, 3.4 strokes per hole and on the par 5's it's 7.0 and on the par 4's it's 4.6, I can see that I'm having the most trouble (the most above par) on the par 5's, then the par 4's, then the par 3's.

Golf Shot Tracker

Par 5's	Actual # Shots	Total Shots	Average
Game 1	5	5	5.00
Game 2	7	12	6.00
Game 3	8	20	6.66
Game 4	7	27	6.75
Game 5	8	35	7.00
Par 4's			
Game 1	5	5	5.00
Game 2	4	9	4.50
Game 3	4	13	4.33
Game 4	6	19	4.75
Game 5	4	23	4.60
Par 3's			
Game 1	3	3	3.00
Game 2	3	6	3.00
Game 3	4	10	3.33
Game 4	3	13	3.25
Game 5	4	17	3.40

Now, dissecting the scorecards even further, I can break my score down into number of fairways hit with my drives, number of greens hit with my approach shots, and number of putts. If there's a total of 18 fairways that can be hit with drives (and second shots on par 5's), by my detailed scorekeeping I can determine how many fairways, on average, I actually hit. Further, I can determine how many greens I hit when I'm within distance of the green—there will be 18 of those too—and I'll be able to determine how many putts I take, on average, per hole, by dividing my total number of putts by 18 holes.

Golf Scorecard - Par 5

Date	Total (5)	Putts (2)	Drives (1)	Fairway (1)	Approach (1)
Apr 10	5	2	1	1	1
Apr 22	7	3	1	2	1
Apr 23	8	3	2	2	1
Apr 30	7	3	2	1	1
May 10	8	2	2	2	2

With this data, I'll be able to better see where I'm having my most trouble in relationship to shooting par golf.

Let's say that through my scorekeeping I find that my putting's about right—just a little above the two putts "par golf" allows per hole—but I only average hitting 10 of 18 fairways and just 8 of 18 greens.

What does that scorekeeping tell me? It tells me if I want to

Golf Scorecard You Carry

Hole	1	2	3	4	5	6	7	8	9	10	11	12	13	14	15	16	17	18	Total
Par	4	3	4	4	5	3	4	5	4	3	4	4	5	3	4	4	5	4	72
Putts	2	3	1	3	2	3	3	2	1	2	3	2	3	3	2	1	3	1	40
Apprch	1	2	1	1	2	1	1	2	2	2	1	1	2	1	1	1	2	1	25
Drives	1	0	1	2	1	0	2	1	1	0	2	1	2	0	2	2	2	2	21
Fairway					1			2					1				1		5/87

lower my score, I need to hit the ball straighter. It says my putting's OK, but I'm spraying the ball too much. I'm not hitting enough fairways and, especially, not enough greens. Nothing complicated about that. And it's probably something I might have suspected. But now I know it.

Armed with this valuable information, *now* I'm in a position to set a reasonable goal for myself. If I can hit two more fairways per round, and four more greens, I should be able to knock four strokes, on the average, off my score.

So that becomes my first goal: hit 12 fairways a round instead of 10, and 12 greens instead of 8, and average 86 strokes per 18 holes instead of 90.

Thus, shooting 86 becomes my new goal, and it is a much more realistic one than simply "shooting 80." If I really want to shoot 80, I better dig deeper and find out where I can cut off more strokes. Maybe shooting 80 can remain a long-range goal, but in the meantime I'll work on a realistic goal.

Thanks to my scorecards, I know that if I'll go to the driving range and work on straightening out my woods and my irons, I'll be working on the right thing. And if I put in enough time and practice, I'll theoretically be able to make my goal—a goal that only became worthwhile and a motivator to me as a golfer after it was stamped "realistic" and "makeable" by my scorekeeping. Only by creating scorecards that helped me see where I stood could I set goals for my game that made sense.

In a very real sense, everything in our businesses, as well as those recreational pursuits we choose to undertake, can be similarly mapped and plotted. We simply need to follow the formula: Scorekeeping first. Then goal-setting.

Two More Strides

Remember the movie *Chariots of Fire*? It won the Oscar for Best Picture of the Year in 1981 for its moving portrayal of a pair of runners on the 1924 British Olympic team, Harold Abrahams and Eric Liddell, who went to the Paris Olympics and won gold medals.

For Abrahams, the story centers around his dogged determination to overcome serious setbacks early in his training that seem to suggest his career as a runner might be anything but triumphant. Despite obvious natural ability, his problem is that he can't seem to come through in the important races. He's lacking something, he's just not sure what.

Then a man named Sam Mussabini, a world-class track coach, comes to the rescue by figuring out what Abrahams is doing wrong: his strides are too long.

The coach calculates that Abrahams takes 50 strides during a 100-meter race and he is overstriding an average of two inches per stride. If he'll put in two more strides, he can win the Olympics.

The point is, only after the coach "scores" Abrahams's running does he approach the sprinter and suggest to him just what he thinks he's capable of achieving and where his goals can realistically be set. The coach doesn't tell the athlete, "Just run faster," he first tells him how to run faster.

In the end, because of their attention to detail, Harold Abrahams is able to finish ahead of four favored American sprinters and win the gold medal. Sam Mussabini, and good scorekeeping, found him those two more steps.

Two More Sales

While Hollywood has yet to make an Academy Award-winning movie about what happened to real estate agent Barbara Knewitz, the results are, in their own way, equally as triumphant as *Chariots of Fire*.

Barbara was frustrated to the point of leaving the real estate business when she came in contact with Chuck Acklin, a GAME OF WORK colleague who convinced her that what she needed wasn't a change of jobs, but a change in keeping score.

First, Chuck asked Barbara a series of questions. How many calls or contacts did it require for her to get an appointment? How many appointments were needed to generate a sale? How many cold calls were necessary before she could expect a positive response?

When, to each of these questions, Barbara answered honestly, "I don't know," Chuck suggested, "Why don't we find out?"

As coach and player, they set up a simple scorekeeping system that called for Barbara to chart her calls, contacts, appointments, sales, and closings. For the first time, she could see just how many calls and contacts were needed to generate the results she was after. More importantly, she was able to see the importance of developing the contacts and relationships that resulted in productive appointments. Through scorekeeping, she was able to see a cause and effect between quality relationships and sales results, and that's where she determined she needed to place her emphasis.

Just as I did when I dissected my golf game to see where I needed to improve in order to realize my goal of shooting a lower overall score, Barbara dissected her real estate business to see where she needed to improve in order to realize her goal of increased sales.

Within two months after implementing her new real estate personal scorecards, Barbara realized an increase in her production of 114 percent. Over the final three months of the year, during the sales period that is traditionally the slowest for selling real estate, she had more sales than the rest of the year combined. She'd always had her goals in mind, but it took a scorecard to make those goals realistic and to bring into focus exactly how to achieve them.

The Concepts of
Scorekeeping

WELL WORTH
THE TIME

*Meaningful scorekeeping
takes no time at all.*

Common Sense Coaching

Imagine a golf course where they tell everyone to stop keeping score. The rational is not only will that speed up play, but more golfers will be able to get on the course—and that will result in a much better realization of the land given to the golf course.

How would golfers react?

They'd think the people running the golf course had lost their minds.

But in business, isn't that exactly what we do? We say we don't have time to keep score, we've gotta work. We hear, "Do you want me to keep track of it, or do you want me to do more of it?"

The truth is, scorekeeping means we can do more of both.

Our GAME OF WORK promise is that you will get considerably more accomplished in a day if you take fifteen minutes of that day to keep score than you will accomplish if you don't. We call it the "15 Minute Rule." It's not an option, it's a rule. An ironclad Gotta-do-it.

Doing Your Homework

People in sports are always showing us the importance of taking time to pay attention to the scorecard. We see it at the end of football and basketball games when coaches "work the clock." We see it in baseball, when coaches change their line-ups or alter their strategies as the competition progresses. All these changes are responses to that quick glance, that brief observation, of just what the score is—and what action might be required as a result.

In a thrilling Tour de France bicycle race in 1990, American Greg LeMond won the race with a stirring come-from-behind sprint on the final day in Paris. LeMond pushed his bicycle to an average speed of 35 miles an hour on the final stretch

People in sports are always showing us the importance of taking time to pay attention to the scorecard.

down the Champs-Elysées and wound up beating Laurent Fignon of France by eight seconds. After racing more than 2,000 miles through five countries in twenty-one days in the most grueling bicycle race in the world, they finished within just eight seconds of each other.

As the race came to the outskirts of Paris prior to the twenty-first and final leg that would start the next morning, LeMond, who had spent most of the race furiously trying to catch Fignon, was almost totally spent. On the verge of exhaustion, he was still behind the leader by fifty seconds, a formidable deficit in bicycling measurements.

But what he did next, in spite of that exhaustion, is what can be especially instructive to those of us interested in constructing effective scorekeeping systems.

Instead of collapsing into bed, LeMond and his coaches took the time to measure where they stood and what they needed to do to catch Fignon in the next day's time trial that would conclude the race. They calculated exactly how much time they were behind Fignon, and what LeMond had to do if he hoped to overtake the leader the next day. No inch of the final route was left unscrutinized.

To help them set their strategy, the members of Team LeMond had all sorts of scorecards in front of them—Fignon's usual time trial times, LeMond's usual time trial times, the topography of the route, where the smart places were to attack, and so on. They set up intermediate split times that LeMond would have to make, and they factored in a cushion for error. Well before LeMond got in the saddle the next day, he knew what hundreds of thousands of Frenchmen hoping for their countryman Fignon did not know: that LeMond had a chance to win.

Greg LeMond never would have known that if he and his team hadn't taken the time the night before to look at their scorecards and form their game plan accordingly. Taking their "15 minutes" definitely set the stage for victory.

Know Your Indicators

In business these days, we're living in a very disciplined, very goal-aware era. Time management is a big item, as are personal self-awareness and prioritization. There are entire companies now whose whole focus is toward helping us schedule our time and set our goals. We can easily spend hundreds and thousands of dollars simply on products that help us "get it together." All of this increased understanding and organization *can* be very valuable. But how often is it?

The problem with the majority of the time-management programs is that they get us to make highly organized lists of our schedules and our goals. But in spite of that, many times we find we're not any closer to our lifetime goals at the end of the year than we were when we started. Too often, we're so busy being busy that we don't take the time to track how we're doing.

It isn't enough just to be well organized and prioritized. We also need to be able to gauge how we're doing. We need a scoreboard.

For every one of us, there are indicators of our progress that we need to be well aware of. I don't care what self-motivation or self-management principles we want to use to be successful at meeting our goals, we need to keep in touch with that indicator. That means we need a scorecard that accurately measures our performance against our predetermined goals and destinations. I can sit down and make prioritized decisions, I can do all the time management steps, I can know where I'll be and who I'll be with and what I'll be doing every quarter hour of every day. But the real evaluation is whether at the end of the year I'm closer to where I said I wanted to be. Am I really reaching my goals, or am I just more organized but still pretty much where I've always been?

To get that evaluation, I need to look at my scorecards, whatever they track. I need to observe the "15 Minute Rule" every day. I need to make sure I take the time to keep score. Maybe I'm a manager over dozens or hundreds, maybe I'm a player managing only myself. That doesn't matter. What does matter is that whatever my role is, I need to make sure I take those fifteen minutes so I can gauge where I stand, and where I stand in relationship to where I've been and where I want to go.

Is it difficult to take those fifteen minutes? Is it a pain? Not at all—because by giving ourselves that self-feedback we wind up with more productivity, and as a result of that, much more energy. Why wouldn't we want to? That's a better question. It's like exercise. Even though it's time spent away from being "on task," it is nonetheless more valuable than if we had stayed on task and never taken such a beneficial break.

It's important, too, that we take care of the fifteen minutes when it's necessary, not just when it's convenient.

With the right kind of scorekeeping in place, we have access to

> **I**t isn't enough just to be well organized and prioritized. We need to be able to gauge how we are doing. We need a scoreboard.

a constant barometer keeping us abreast of the current, as well as the final, score. We need to look at that barometer, that scoreboard, on a regular basis. We need to set up a scorekeeping system that gives us information when we need it—so we can use it to our advantage along the way.

All I Ask Is 15 Minutes a Day

At a supermarket chain we worked with in the Pacific Northwest, they put the daily "15 Minute Rule" to the test in their deli departments. Management set up scorecards that separated sales into two shifts, one that ended at four o'clock in the afternoon and the other that started at four o'clock. There was nothing magical about four o'clock. It just happened to be where management made the split.

The scorecards, which they took care to update every day, were simple and to-the-point, charting just what you'd expect in a supermarket delicatessen—sales of sandwiches, chips, pickles, slices of cheesecake, and so forth, as well as the total number of customers who came through the deli.

The positive results in productivity driven by these scorecards were dramatic. By simply taking fifteen minutes a day to set up and maintain these scorecards, sales at the chain's delicatessens skyrocketed. Not only did the workers know what their volume was yesterday, but they knew what the volume was yesterday of the "other" shift. The competition that naturally sprang up between the before-four and after-four shifts greatly enhanced player buy-in and, as a direct result, productivity.

In another example, a general contractor who had been in business more than twenty-five years accepted the principle of a few minutes of scorekeeping each day and decided to track the company's average daily bank balance. This took less than five minutes a day.

Looking at the balance with this frequency, the chief financial officer reached a new level of understanding about the company's collection and payment departments. As a result, the company was able to fine tune its collections and payments schedules and realize an increase in interest earnings of more than $100,000 a year.

Make Scorekeeping Your Top Priority

Taking the time to keep score is a matter of priority. When it is seen as valuable, finding the time becomes automatic. You'll short-change something else before you'll break your commitment to the 15 Minute Rule and daily scorekeeping.

How to do it? Let me illustrate. Let's say I'm a department manager for a large chain of retail stores and I've got a dozen stores I need to visit every month. Let's also say as a company we've set a target sales goal of realizing one dollar per customer visit. We've decided that expenditure-per-customer is one of the key ways we want to keep score.

Now I can use all my time to get in my car and systematically visit each of the stores for which I'm responsible. That's pretty much standard operating procedure for sales managers, right?

Or, I can use my scorekeeping system and look at the score-cards from my dozen stores and let them help me decide where my attention is needed; where I can do the most good. I can set aside those "15 minutes" every workday and tally up how we're doing. I can look at the departments that are generating their dollar per customer, and then some, and leave them with a "congratulations and keep up the good work." I can look at those departments that may be coming up short, and probe the scorecards further to find out why, whether it's a scheduling problem or a motivation problem or something else that's going on. Whatever it is, that is where I'll turn my attention. It might mean I get to one less store, or spend a little less time driving around, but the return on my time investment will be far greater.

Make It Yours!

It requires a good deal of discipline to stop what we're doing long enough so we can *see* what we're doing. Human nature is to keep running, churning, moving. The goal line is ahead and who wants to stop? It's not just the defense who calls the time out; the offense benefits from them too.

What we fail to realize is that the occasional pause from activity to assess and evaluate just what is going on can be most beneficial to the overall journey. The time spent keeping score will pay untold dividends, paving the way for focus and clarity otherwise obscured by the constant motion of the endeavor. Take enough time to create and maintain your scorecards. The pause you take will catapult you and your company to success.

The Concepts of
Scorekeeping

KEEP IT POSITIVE

*Reinforce the behavior
you want repeated*

Common Sense Coaching

*P*ause *for a moment and think about your business, or your family. Now think about what percentage of the time you and/or your team are doing it right. What percentage of the time do you do whatever you do correctly? Whether it's answer the phone, change a diaper, take out the garbage, fill an order, ship a product, give medication in a hospital, bandage a scraped knee, take and fill a fastfood order, mow the lawn; whatever you do, what percentage of the time do you do it right? Is it 90 percent, 95 percent? Maybe 99 percent?*

Now think about what you get the majority of your feedback on? Is it on what you do right? Or, in your situation, as is so often the case, does the majority of your feedback focus on not only the things you don't want to repeat but on the things you didn't want to have happen in the first place: the mistakes, the errors, the oversights, the foul-ups. These are the fumbles that make up a very small percentage of your overall performance. The things you do wrong.

What is it about our society that causes us to violate the most fundamental principle in all of human behavior—that we want to reinforce the behavior that we want repeated?

Custom-made Scorecards

How do we go about this business of reinforcing behavior we want repeated? How do we accentuate the positive?

The answer: by proactively creating appropriate scorecards.

As we've discussed, traditional ways of measuring, or keeping track, usually just don't get the job done. Most of us have learned that through sad experience. Counting our mistakes fails to motivate us for a number of reasons, and chiefly because we don't have a clear picture of what we're doing right.

It's when we create and customize our own scorecards that we are then able to put the emphasis where we want it, and where it belongs.

To illustrate this point, I like the story of Tyler Williams. Tyler is the son of Rick Williams, a GAME OF WORK colleague with whom I collaborated on the book, *Managing The Obvious*.

When he turned twelve, Tyler joined a junior basketball league. His father was hopeful that his son's first encounter with organized sports would be a positive experience. But Rick had his doubts. As a soccer referee, Rick had all too often seen the psychological and emotional damage that could be inflicted on young athletes by coaches, parents, officials, and so on, simply by accentuating the negative.

In his determination to not be a part of a process that might be in any way counterproductive, and to help ensure his son's enjoyment of what he knew would be a most competitive process (even if the kids were only 12), Rick set out to formulate a plan that would focus only on the positive.

Which is how he happened to come up with his "Parent's Scorecard."

Rick's scorecard tracked a wide variety of tangible contributions to the team cause, including points, rebounds, assists, steals, blocked shots, times Tyler passed the ball, and broken-up passes. During Tyler's games, Rick would sit on the sidelines and make a mark on his Parent's Scorecard every time Tyler made one of these positive "contributions." At the end of the game, he would tally up all of these contribution points. It was a simple process. If Tyler had three points, four rebounds, three assists, one blocked shot, two steals and two broken-up passes in a game, that would add up to 15 contribution points.

Tyler's Scorecard

Game	Points	Rebound	Assist	Steal	Blocked Shot	Pass	Broken Up Pass	TOTAL
1	III	IIII	III	II	I		II	15
2								

Rick's original intent for his Parent's Scorecard was to make sure that he, as a parent, would stay focused on the positive things Tyler was doing during his basketball games. By being occupied on the sidelines, and by purposely avoiding scoring anything negative, such as turnovers, missed shots, bad passes, fouls, and so on, Rick reasoned that he could avoid the pitfalls of youth league negativity.

As the season wore on, Rick noticed that not only was his scorecard keeping him busy, but that Tyler's own interest in his "contribution points" grew with each game.

Whereas the statistics kept by the coaches centered chiefly on points and rebounds—the two traditional forms of measurement used in junior basketball—Tyler's Dad's scorecards awarded points for virtually everything positive accomplished during the game.

Tyler's Expanded Scorecard

Game	Points	Rebound	Assist	Steal	Blocked Shot	Pass	Broken Up Pass	TOTAL
1	III	IIII	III	II	I		II	15
2	I	III	IIII	III	I	II		14
3		IIII	HHT	III	II	IIII		18
4	II	III	HHT	II	III	II	III	20
5	III	II	III	IIII	HHT	III	II	22
6	III	II	II	III	III	IIII	I	18
7	IIII	IIII	III	III	HHT	III	I	23
8	HHT I	III	II	IIII	III	III	III	24
9	HHT	IIII	III	III	II	IIII	IIII	25

It wasn't long before Tyler was sprinting over to where his Dad sat during timeouts, to check on his contribution points, before reporting to the team huddle. When they reached home after the game, Tyler would hustle to his bedroom, where he had a scorecard on the wall that plotted his contribution point progress. With a simple dot line on a graph Tyler had made himself, he could see whether he was improving. As the season progressed, the line on his graph went steadily upward. Without a single chewing-out session or unpleasant experience, Tyler turned into a better basketball player, and enjoyed the process besides.

Tyler's Contribution Points

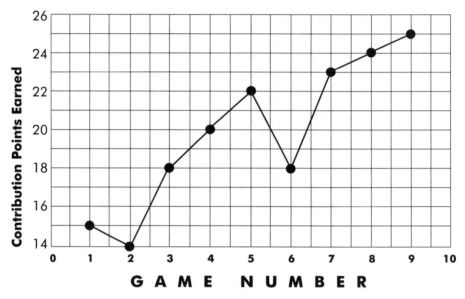

It was because of the information produced by Rick's tailor-made scoresheets that Tyler was able to gauge his progress and make improvements in areas that would have otherwise been obscure to him, at best. Left to determine his performance according to the team's scorekeeping only, unless he was the top scorer and rebounder, he would have been faced with regular reminders of what he *wasn't* doing. But armed with his own "stats," he could see clearly his personal progress. Through the use of a personalized scorekeeping system that allowed him to see exactly where he was improving, Tyler was able to clearly identify his course and find his way to success, which could be defined as both improving as a basketball player in his personal skills and in his contributions to the team.

As a postscript to the Tyler Williams story, Rick Williams reported that he got a phone call not long after telling his Parent's Scorecard story at a GAME OF WORK seminar. The call was from a man who had been in the audience and, after hearing Rick's story, said he wanted more details. He explained that he was an official of a youth basketball league that was having problems with what he called "spectator negativity."

Rick gladly supplied him with a working model of the parent's scorecard and the league instituted a program where every player was assigned his or her own scorekeeper in the stands. The official later reported that parental sideline abuse came to a screeching halt as a result. The scorecards helped the players become better at basketball, and helped their league become better as well.

Workplace Application

Now you're probably thinking, "That's a fine story about Tyler Williams. His father's scorecard helped him reinforce behavior any basketball player would want to repeat. But is what worked for a twelve year old playing basketball going to work in the tough, no-nonsense business place? Can it survive in that kind of a competitive atmosphere? Can it survive at MY company?"

The answer is absolutely.

A few years ago, I got a call from an executive in Arizona whose business was having trouble controlling what retail businesses refer to as warehouse damage and truck shorts, that is, product that is lost, damaged, stolen, or otherwise unaccounted for in the order and delivery process.

"Of thirty-two warehouses in our company, mine ranks the worst in warehouse damage and truck shorts," said the executive, who then added, "I want to see if your stuff works. See what you can do."

For incentive, he offered to refer our services to every other warehouse in the company chain if we were successful.

Now that he had our attention, we dug our heels in and went to work.

Our challenge was to design a scorecard that would identify areas of contribution that would help reduce the damage and shorts. Just like Rick Williams with his basketball-playing son, our objective was to see how we might best identify those areas that would motivate the warehouse "players" to improve their levels of performance.

> **O**ur challenge was to design a scorecard that would identify areas of contribution.

First we took a look at the way the company was currently measuring warehouse performance and shrink (loss due to damage, theft, spoilage, etc.). Not surprisingly, the traditional accounting department's measurements were not dynamic. They tended to be after the fact, and, worst of all, they took in such a large block of time and such a large amount of product that they gave off the impression that the problem was just too big to solve.

The loss due to warehouse damage and truck shorts was not

insignificant. It amounted to a little over a quarter of a million dollars every month. More than $3 million a year! As a result, everyone involved had arrived at the conclusion that it was a problem too big for them to solve. "It's beyond us!" was the party line, and that empowered the players to come up with plenty of macro-economic excuses, like it was the fault of the weather, or the governor, and sometimes even the president.

Our challenge was obvious. We needed to create a scorekeeping system that would take the problem down to the player's level—so that the players in the warehouse could relate and identify with the dollar amount lost or saved each month.

We implemented daily scorecards that concentrated on the three areas of accountability—warehouse damage, truck shorts, and total system shrink. But instead of monitoring how much product was getting damaged, or lost, or stolen, our measurements were on the amount of product that was delivered in good shape, on time, and totally accounted for. Positive scorekeeping had just entered the warehouse.

The scorecards we created were aimed at reinforcing the behavior we wanted repeated. Not what we didn't want repeated.

The results were dramatic. In the first year alone the warehouse team was able to reduce the $3 million shrink by almost a million dollars. Subsequent year's results have continued to improve to the point that losses due to warehouse damage and truck shorts were reduced to less than one-sixteenth of their previous level. After seven years under the "new positive scorekeeping system," more than $10 million had been saved.

Counting Safety, Not Accidents

In sharp contrast to positive-oriented scorekeeping, consider that OSHA, the arm of the federal government that monitors safe working conditions in America's businesses and factories, uses a measuring statistic with the acronym AFR, which stands for Accident Frequency Report.

Companies are required to periodically report to OSHA the number of accidents per so many thousand labor hours worked. Each company then gets an AFR rate, which is calculated mathematically and reported in decimal format, meaning the final AFR is going to wind up being something like .231, .162, or some such figure.

Now I'll guarantee you that 95 percent of the businesses in America don't have a clue what AFR means, much less what they can do about it or if they're winning or losing. Put simply, no one cares.

The AFR is a classic example of emphasizing the negative … and getting negative results in return.

You can look around the marketplace and see many more examples of negative measurement every day. Instance after instance where what's kept track of are errors, tardies, complaints, liabilities, collisions. The negatives. Company personnel files are either empty or full of petty little complaint reports on an employee, whether from a client, a colleague or a supervisor. Yearly evaluation forms are vague, subjective and sometimes padded to reflect whatever the supervisor wants to emphasize.

But for every negative there's a positive. Where there are tardies, complaints, and so forth, there should also be just the opposite— on-times, compliments, etc. Chart the scorecard on those opposites. Keep score on the positives.

A major manufacturer of defense equipment for the United States government learned this lesson firsthand when management changed its approach to the problem of employee absenteeism.

For years, the company had wrestled with lost productivity due to what was seen as a chronic attendance problem. On average, anywhere from three to six percent of the work force would miss work each day. In a company with over 6,000 employees, that amounted to a lot of labor hours lost, and productivity took a major hit as a result.

Try as it might, the company couldn't manage to reduce its absenteeism. Threats and lectures didn't work. Corrective actions for the biggest abusers failed to appreciably shift the percentages. If anything, as time went on and frustration mounted, the problem only got worse.

Then the company did an about-face. Instead of keeping score on its absenteeism, it began keeping score on what it called "presenteeism." It kept track of who was at work instead of who wasn't.

In place of regular reports that reflected an absentee rate ranging from 3 to 6 percent, now the reports trotted out to the troops showed a presentee rate of 94 to 97 percent.

With that kind of positive emphasis in place, the next thing the company did was offer incentives to its employees to elevate presenteeism higher. Free lunches for entire departments were offered, along with other department-wide bonuses. Getting to 98 percent, or 99 percent, or even 100 percent, became an opportunity instead of an obligation. It was something to celebrate instead of something to worry about. Rather than punishing offenders, the new attitude rewarded those who got the job done.

The results were as gratifying as they were dramatic. The players themselves began disciplining those among them who failed to show up for work. A team spirit developed for being on the job. Presenteeism shot up across the board, from a low of 94 percent, when the change in reporting took place, to nearly 99 percent a little over three years later.

Make It Yours!

There's a magic that happens when we concentrate on the good that is being done and encourage that kind of performance. Whether it's in our business or our personal life, emphasizing the positive can have a profound effect. Scorecards that focus on the positive will yield positive results. And vice versa. Take the challenge to build your own scorecards that will, as with young Tyler Williams, propel you to progress and succeed. Concentrate your efforts on the positive.

There's a magic that happens when we concentrate on the good that is being done and encourage that kind of performance.

The Concepts of Scorekeeping

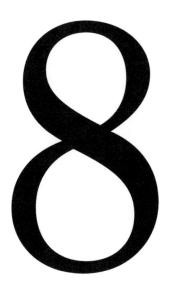

COACH AND PLAYER

The primary reason for scorekeeping is to allow coach and player to agree on when, what type, and how much feedback is appropriate.

Common Sense Coaching

How does a PGA golfer know when he needs to go see his instructor? How does a baseball batting leader know when it's time to be videotaped and receive a coach's appraisal? How does a top-ranked tennis professional know it's time for a training session with his or her coach? When the scores fall. That's how. When the averages dip. When the percentage of first serves drops. In virtually every recreational endeavor, the willingness of the player to be coached and the necessity for that player to seek coaching is dictated by what is communicated by a carefully detailed scorecard.

When Andre Agassi fails to get past the first round in four consecutive tournaments, he seeks out his coach; and when he does he's going to be coachable and humble, because he knows he needs it. When a batting champion in baseball sees his percentage drop five or ten points over several games, he doesn't wait for the month-end report in order to know that he needs help. He and his coach will be in the batting cage or going over videotape early the next morning. By the same token, when that batter has an outstanding streak of hits, his coach knows it's time to leave well enough alone. If it ain't broke, don't fix it.

The Value of the Coach-Player Relationship

Michael Jordan made what many considered an unusually resolute demand after he and his team, the Chicago Bulls, won their fifth professional basketball championship. The man regarded as basketball's greatest player told the team's owners that if they didn't keep head coach Phil Jackson, who was involved at the time in a contract dispute with management, then he wouldn't play for the Bulls the next season.

Most members of the media considered Jordan's statement a

bluff. How could someone who was making over $30 million a year just walk away? How could a coach possibly mean that much?

But the Bulls' owners knew their star player wasn't bluffing. A month after Jordan's ultimatum, Coach Jackson had a new contract. For $6 million.

What Michael Jordan, with a championship ring for every finger *and* the thumb, appreciated enough to quit over was the tremendous value of a good relationship between a player and a coach.

In sports, it's easy for players and coaches to quantify the value of their relationship. The reason, of course, is scorekeeping. Championships won, statistical titles, records, personal best performances, and so on, are all plotted, calculated and measured from every direction. Scorecards are everywhere, and they accurately tell the tale for both coach and player. They reflect what works and what doesn't. When John Elway, the longtime quarterback for the Denver Broncos, went through a change of coaches and said that the change was a good one for him, he wasn't basing that on any kind of subjective reasoning. He was basing it on the fact that it took him ten years to throw for three thousand yards under the old coach, and under the new coaches, he gained three thousand passing yards in half that time. His completion percentage, interception ratio, and overall quarterback rating went up as well. All anyone had to do was look at the scorecards. It was all right there.

What happens if we have those kinds of scorecards in place where we work? Guesswork, for one thing, would go out the window, and so would popularity contests and other forms of favoritism that provide inequitable rewards.

With a definitive scorecard in place that both coach and player agree on, the result is a clear and objective picture to look at. The scorecard gives the player (worker/employee/trainee) and the coach (manager/supervisor/boss) the data they need to communicate based on reality instead of perception and fantasy.

It's when coach and player work together that the scorecard is at its most useful and powerful.

It's when coach and player work together that the scorecard is at its most useful and powerful. That's when coach and player find themselves in a position to first, agree on the most important things the player does to benefit the company, and second, make sure working, credible, positive scorecards are put in place, and are constantly revised to measure the player's progress in those areas.

The beauty of the scorecard process is that it enables both coach and player to not only get on the same page, but to sort through all the extraneous, irrelevant baggage and actually arrive at what is most important. That kind of same-wavelength communication is amazingly valuable. Knowing what your boss, or coach, is thinking is imperative to making progress.

It has long been my experience that the following corollary is true:

People succeed in business in direct relationship to how well they take over their boss's job!

I don't mean that literally, of course. What I do mean is that it is vitally important for a player to understand what the coach needs most—and then give it to him or her. Help the coach get his or her job done. That's where success begins. That's how we make progress within an organization, and that is how an organization increases productivity.

Isn't that what happens in games? When Michael Jordan goes onto a basketball court and runs the triangle offense exactly as ordered by Phil Jackson, isn't Michael Jordan in essence taking over the boss's job?

It was Vince Lombardi, the legendary football coach, who reportedly was the first to say, "It's amazing how much better I coach when I have good players."

One question we get asked frequently at THE GAME OF WORK is, "OK, I understand I need to communicate with my coach and keep score on the most important things I do that benefit my company. But where do I start? And how many of these things should I actually keep score on?"

That's an important question because it addresses the fact that we can't possibly keep score on *everything*. We need to prioritize. We need to make sure we not only follow the "15 Minute Rule," and not exceed it, but we need to take care that we use those minutes effectively.

That's why we recommend keeping score on the top five things you do to benefit your company.

Look at your list of priorities and concentrate on knowing the score on the first five.

How do you score those top five? For help with that, just turn on TV during the World Series.

Have you noticed all the numbers that typically come on the television screen when a player comes to bat in the Series? Sometimes you can barely see the player's face for all the numbers or stats that are listed: his batting average, his slugging percentage, his on-base percentage, how many steals he averages per game, how many walks per game, his batting average against righthanders, against lefthanders, on days it rains, on days it doesn't rain. Then they duplicate everything to differentiate between regular season stats and World Series stats.

It's the same thing in a basketball game when a player is getting ready to shoot a free throw. They'll flash on the TV screen his rebounding averages, his scoring averages, his assists average, his steals average. They'll show his shooting percentages for regular shots, for three-point shots and for foul shots. They'll show how many minutes he plays per game, they'll differentiate between regular season and play-off games, and so on.

In football, they'll zoom in on the quarterback and show graphics of how many passes he completes per game, how many yards those passes average, how many yards per game he averages running, how many times he's been intercepted, and the list goes on.

Name a sport, any sport, and what do we see? We see statistics from scorecards that are set up for the specific purpose of identifying the most important things the athletes do. In tennis, it's first-serve percentage and number of unforced errors; in golf, it's everything from driving distance to putts-per-round to greens-in-regulation to sand saves; in volleyball, it's kills and digs and spikes.

It's certainly not difficult for any of the players involved in these games to know what the top things are to keep score on; it's no question for them to know how to win. In the world of games, each player is well aware of what it is that he or she is expected to contribute.

Imagine if Michael Jordan went into Phil Jackson's office and said, "Coach, I want you to help me identify the five most important things I do for this team, and I want to develop a scorecard for them."

Jackson might say, "Well Michael, the five most important things I need you to do for this team are score points, pull down rebounds, hand out assists, steal the ball, and play good defense on the opposing team's shooting guard."

After identifying the five most important things, it would then be up to Jordan and Jackson to develop a way to keep score that would monitor just how well Jordan was doing in those areas. In basketball, of course, such a scoresheet already exists. The standard "box score" keeps track of everything listed above, plus quite a bit more. In reality, Jordan and Jackson wouldn't have to have this conversation. They already have a system that keeps coach and player together.

Manage Better with Scorecards

Unfortunately, many businesses aren't like a basketball team; they don't operate with a scorecard already in place. Many businesses and organizations still operate, however unintentionally, under the principle of the squeaky wheel getting the grease. Too often, the performer who just gets his or her job done without a lot of flash, without a lot of attitude, without a lot of hand-holding and coddling from management, gets overlooked. Lost in the crowd. Management notices the complainers, the squeakers. The employee who shouts the loudest gets noticed. It's human nature.

But that doesn't have to be the case if we listen instead to our scorecards. Not if we look at the "stats" and find out what the score really is.

Consider what happened with a grocery store manager we worked with after he implemented reliable scorecards in his store—the kind that allowed everyone involved to identify their most important areas of contribution and, at the same time, illuminate the producers from the non-producers.

For years, this manager, not unlike most grocery store managers, had operated under the impression that the produce department manager, who had to deal with a highly perishable product, was of great value to the business. Based on perception of importance, the produce manager was paid a premium wage and was considered an integral part of the management team. He or she would routinely have input in key managerial decisions and would typically be invited to upper-level staff retreats and to participate in incentive programs.

By contrast, the person in charge of the frozen food department, located right next to the produce department, had always been viewed as expendable. Because frozen foods were essentially non-perishable (barring power failure), the person in charge of frozen foods did not enjoy anything approaching esteemed status, and certainly had nothing close to the stature enjoyed by the produce manager.

Then this manager completed a GAME OF WORK training program on the value of scorekeeping. He decided to set up scorecards and check out just who was producing what in his store.

Guess what the manager discovered when he applied his new profitability-per-customer scorecard, as generated by the store's computer system, to the produce manager and the clerk running the frozen foods?

He discovered that frozen foods was actually doing a better, more efficient job than produce. The scorecards allowed the manager to see that just because the produce manager was part of the store's "elite," and just because that department enjoyed a historically high profile in the industry, the person who was really producing for the company, and the person the company needed to pay more attention to, in terms of compensation and other forms of appreciation, was the frozen food manager. It was the produce manager who needed to score higher and start contributing more to the store's productivity.

The astute manager/coach will accumulate real facts, real information, and then use that real data to do some real coaching.

It all starts with the scorecard.

It isn't easy. Unfortunately, most of us went through all of our college and most of our careers with little training in the area of coaching. We've had courses on managing, controlling, statistical process control, planning, but virtually nonexistent has been the kind of training that allows managers and would-be managers to develop specific one-on-one coaching skills. As a result, most of us don't know how to coach and more importantly, we don't know when.

Scorekeeping is the tool that can teach us how to coach and, in turn, trigger effective coaching.

There is a sore need for good coaching in business today. In response to that need, I believe a coaching revolution of sorts has already begun. It is my view that business is starting to come around, slowly but surely, to the values of sound communication in the workplace. We're beginning to realize that while we may use up to 25 or 35 percent of our base wage cost in fringe benefits such as sick leave, vacation, and 401K's—all of which you have to be off the job to enjoy—the real potential for mega returns on our investment exists in the simple truth that **the way people feel about an organization is primarily dictated by the way they feel about their coach.**

A divisional director may be earning six-digit bonuses and still feel underappreciated because his or her coach didn't call. But an entry-level worker at a fast food restaurant will feel ultimately empowered because the manager, who may be only weeks older

The way people feel about an organization is primarily dictated by the way they feel about their coach.

64

than the employee, has learned how to make people feel important. The principle is the same: people will rise to the levels that are perceived for them.

Make It Yours!

There's a coaching gap-osis running rampant in our society. Too many managers don't know how to coach, and most people don't know how to ask for coaching. We've got a whole lot of "Don't ask, don't tell" out there. Don't ask for coaching because it's not considered "cool," and don't give hands-on coaching because we're afraid we'll appear condescending. We're afraid of the consequences of coaching; we're afraid we might set a dangerous precedent if we give too much of it; we're afraid of what we might hear.

We need to embrace coaching instead of turn away from it. The relationship between a coach and a player is absolutely essential to the scorekeeping process. It is THE ingredient that not only makes scorekeeping necessary, but that makes it work. Remember, every day when we go to work, each one of us wants to know, *How do I win?* Remember, too, that none of us can find out unless we're willing to listen to the exchange of feedback between coach and player.

Take the time to identify your coach. List how you know you are winning. Describe in a sentence how your coach lets you know you are winning. Create strategies you can use to let your team know how they are winning.

And just a note about uncooperative coaches. Ideally, your coach would be introducing you to this wonderful concept of scorekeeping. You would then have his or her complete buy-in and commitment. Your coach would let you know how to help him or her win, and the alignment would be marvelous. Unfortunately, it is not a perfect world, and many of you will understand the inherent enjoyment of a scorekeeping process before your coach figures it out.

Do not be discouraged. We have secret scorekeepers all over the world. Determine if you were self-employed, how would you decide that you were winning at your job? Go from there. Or even better yet, imagine that you have your boss's job. Now, how would you tell you what winning was? Do this exercise often enough, follow through on your scorecards, and you will have your boss's job.

9

CELEBRATE

A good system has more celebration than excuse-making.

Common Sense Coaching

Victories in life are always accompanied by the appropriate cel-ebration. Whether it's a ticker-tape parade for the first astro-naut, an NBA champion, a World Series winner, the winner of an election, or an impromptu party for the new spelling bee champion of the fourth grade, in our society, accomplishments measured by acceptable scorecards demand celebration.

It's not just the big victories that demand, and result in, cele-bration. We naturally celebrate preliminary and/or intermediate triumphs as well. A home run brings the teammates out of the dugout and fans out of the seats well before the final outcome has been decided. The game-winning bloop single produces the same experience, only more so. In basketball, a high-five is exchanged after every basket or successful free throw. Every level of success in recreation has a prescribed and expected celebration innately linked to it.

We need to incorporate that principle into the scorekeeping we do at work. We need to make sure that our scorekeeping systems have celebration levels prescribed for each level of accomplish-ment. You wouldn't have a ticker-tape parade for a first-inning home run. You certainly don't have the same level of celebration for a hole-in-one by an amateur as you do for a hole-in-one that produces a victory at the Masters. Knowing how much to celebrate is equally as important as knowing when. Good scorekeeping car-ries with it an interrelated level of recognition and reward/celebra-tion. It gives us feedback that lets us know both the how and the when.

Stroke by Stroke

One of the most inspirational stories coming out of the Centennial Olympic Games held in Atlanta involved a 23-year-old American swimmer named Amy Van Dyken. It wasn't just that Van Dyken became the first American woman to win four gold medals in one Olympics in any sport, winter or summer. It wasn't even that Van Dyken suffers from an unrelenting strain of asthma that should have kept her away from racing competitively entirely.

It was the way she celebrated.

Almost daily while the swimming competition was going on, the front page of newspapers from one end of the country to the other would show a picture of Amy Van Dyken, her fist thrust high in the air, and the biggest smile you've ever seen spread from one side of her face to the other.

This athlete knew how to celebrate!

She was the thrill of victory personified; a one-woman Kodak moment. She led group hugs after her wins in the relays, she gleefully tossed her bouquet of flowers into the stands after her triumph in the butterfly, and after she made history with her record-setting fourth gold medal in the 50-meter freestyle race she let out a scream of joy they could hear all the way back in her hometown of Englewood, Colorado.

As Amy soaked it all in, clearly enjoying her "moments," her personal story was told, which helped explain why her celebrations were so heartfelt and personally satisfying. Why they brought her so much unmitigated joy.

She had been born with a particular strain of asthma that left her vulnerable to just about everything. Whereas many asthmatics might have their attacks of breathlessness induced by either allergies, infection, or exercise, Amy's could be induced by all three. Her childhood doctors only allowed her into a swimming pool because they hoped that a little mild exercise, while an enemy to her asthma, would build her up physically to at least help with her stamina. While encouraging her to swim, the doctors also cautioned Amy to take it easy. Just exercise gently, they told her, no serious workouts.

But the unseen, and uncounted-on, variable in the equation was Amy's indomitable spirit. As she would trudge daily to the swimming pool at her neighborhood club in the suburbs of Denver, she would look at the clock on the wall, and at the other kids swimming their races. Slowly but surely, she resolved to get stronger; to swim faster. As a young girl she established her own set of goals, and her own system of scorekeeping.

When she was first able to swim the *width* of the pool, she celebrated.

When she was first able to swim it lengthwise, she celebrated.

When she was finally able to enter a club race—swimming against eight-year-olds when she was fourteen—she celebrated.

The asthma and the allergies never went away, but neither did Amy. Never able to get her breathing beyond 60 percent of the lung capacity of a normal fully grown adult, it took her until the ripe old age of twenty-three, ancient for a competitive female swimmer, to finally qualify for the Olympic Games. At Atlanta, she found herself mostly swimming alongside teenagers.

In the end, she wound up leading them all to the wall. No one in the Olympics swam faster, harder, or with more enthusiasm; no one won as much gold, and, for sure, no one set a better example of how and when to celebrate than Amy Van Dyken. She knew how to do it! When she met her goals, she knew it, and so did everyone else. Wouldn't it be wonderful if in our businesses, and all areas of our lives, we could set up scorecards that allowed us the same levels of motivation and enjoyment?

Opening Doors

We consulted for a time with a large garage door manufacturing company that, after setting up its scorecards, decided to implement what the company called an "awards luncheon" for all its employees. The barbecue lunch, it was decided, would be held every Friday and the company's suppliers, dealers, and any customers who wanted to attend, would also be invited. The purpose of the Friday lunch was to honor anyone who had accomplished their sales goals for the week.

This celebration luncheon was dutifully held every week. Not once in a while. Not some of the time. But every Friday, without fail.

Skeptics were quick to predict that the luncheons would soon get old and lose their appeal. But just the opposite proved to be true. Over time, the Friday luncheons turned from a curious novelty into a tradition where old-timers remembered the earlier luncheons and the new kids, even the Generation X'ers who thought it was kind of hokey at first, began to see the power in the camaraderie generated by this collective celebration.

Most importantly, sales performances continued to increase as both coaches and players raised the level of their productivity.

Besides just keeping score, effective scorekeeping systems provide for appropriate celebration. Care is taken not to overlook the "little" victories that are continually taking place, the kind that might otherwise be overlooked in the fast-paced marketplace.

By designing scorecards that parallel those in athletic contests, we create ample opportunities for appropriate and timely celebration. Just as it doesn't matter what inning it is in a baseball game, or what half in a basketball game, or what period in a hockey game, and just as it doesn't matter what stage of the season it happens to be, if something good happens, it's going to be celebrated. So it can be in business. Whether it's Monday or Friday, July or January, the start of the sales period, the middle, or the end, when good things happen, celebrate.

> **Besides just keeping score, effective scorekeeping systems provide for appropriate celebration.**

Scorecards allow us to make a big deal out of the right stuff we want more of; they allow us to chart people showing up on time (not late, but on time), for meeting that day's quota, for meeting that week's quota, for any number of important productive efforts.

If we have a scorecard that allows us to only celebrate at the end of the year, and there are plenty of them out there, that leaves us with just one opportunity to celebrate. But if we take that same performance measured by that once-a-year scorecard and simply increase the frequency of its measurement, we increase the frequency for celebration. Along the way we will unavoidably decrease excuse-making. For one thing, we're just too busy celebrating.

Make no mistake, in order to be meaningful, the celebrating must be based on hard and tangible data. Not just perceived, subjective data, but real data. We don't name an employee of the month based on nothing, or on the manager's whim. We base it on our scorecard data.

It also follows that when we increase celebration we greatly increase the number of winners. It pays to not just recognize the top seller, the top performer, the top producer, but to recognize all those who, within their spheres and capabilities, exceed the expectations as mandated by their personal scorecards. We're far better off to focus on all employees who go over or who reach some threshold performance, and call that our President's Club or Achiever's Group or some other proclaimed in-crowd, than to focus on just a select few. In so doing, we spur everyone to their best efforts, and greatly increase our reasons to legitimately celebrate and further encourage superior effort.

We need to constantly ask "Who wins in our organizations, in our families?" Do we only give recognition to the child with the best grades, or do we also give recognition to the child whose grades are better than they were in the past? When we have the sales awards and sales contests do we set it up in such a fashion that we take all the money budgeted and plunk it in front of one single "best" performer? Or, do we establish the opportunity for the majority of the people in the sales force, if they're able, to reach a minimum improvement over past performance—so they get to come to the dinner too?

Sales managers over the years seem to be in a never-ending quest for the magic pill or the magic formula. One of the old traditions is the steak and beans dinner. Those salespeople who achieve or lead the sales force get steak served to them and those who fail to lead have to come to the same banquet and eat beans.

But what good does that kind of system honestly effect? What kind of incentive does "eating beans" inspire for the majority who are eating them?

Rather, we champion the kind of productive scorekeeping we saw implemented by a GAME OF WORK manufacturing client that we watched grow from less than a thousand dollars in sales to over a hundred million in revenue in little more than a decade.

This company's key principle was concentrating on maximizing the number of winners.

One of this company's key principles was concentrating on maximizing the number of winners. Management implemented a gain-sharing program where every six months the company would distribute ten percent of its pre-tax profits among all its employees. Unlike many organizations—where the bonus is distributed as a percentage of base salary, thus favoring those making bigger salaries, like upper management—the founder of this organization, in his wisdom, elected to share equally. When the team won, everybody won. Profit was divided by the number of people who had been employed six months or more and everyone received the same dollar amount.

That's maximizing the number of winners to the ultimate. A $1,500 check to an individual making just slightly over minimum wage is a huge reward. And while that same $1,500 may be relatively insignificant, financially speaking, to a CEO or high-level executive, the sense of team is the same and the result is a tremendous morale boost for everyone involved.

The key to remember is that celebration can come in a variety of forms, and it doesn't always have to be big brass bands.

McDonald's, as well as some of our other fine fast-food friends, has long understood the importance of recognizing what might be considered small tasks.

It is possible in the McDonald's Corporation to become certified at each of a number of positions. Running the bin (where the hamburgers slide down), for example, is the real quarterback of any franchise operation and one of the most skilled and demanding of positions. At McDonald's, you can be officially certified as a bin manager. You can also be a certified shake-maker, a certified fryer, a certified grill person, and so on. When you have completed and demonstrated the appropriate skills for your particular assignment, you are rewarded with a uniform patch that announces to the world that you are certified. On the surface, it might seem like a simple thing. But it is with this system that McDonald's succeeds in allowing people to have more than just a job. Systems of recognition always allow people to feel capable, competent, more skilled, and in general better about themselves as well as about where they work.

Make It Yours!

Remember Miami in 1997, right after the Florida Marlins won the World Series? Spontaneous celebrations sprang up all around the city. Every street had a party. A victory parade held in the downtown area was attended by hundreds of thousands.

By contrast, can you imagine the American Management Association's approach to celebrating the World Series, allowing for no advance planning? Wouldn't the thinking be more along the lines of, "We're not at the anniversary date yet so it's not time to give feedback," or, "Nobody scheduled this celebration so we can't get a parade permit."

No one in the world would think of *not* celebrating the World Series victory. Everybody celebrates in sports. And yet, in business, we find non-celebration all the time.

Resolve to create scorecards in your business that promote spontaneous, mandatory, and frequent celebration when it is called for by appropriate triumphs. In your sales force, in your management team, in your customer satisfaction department, whatever area you're involved in, set up scorecards that allow everyone to win and celebrate.

10

MAXIMIZE
THE NUMBER
OF WINNERS

Scorecards need to be based on,
as well as judged by, the players
whose performance they assess.

Common Sense Coaching

Every year in the United States we have dozens of major marathons. It seems that every big city hosts one of these 26.2-mile tests of endurance, and a lot of other cities and towns besides. These marathons attract people from all ages and walks of life, and out of those hundreds of thousands, maybe millions, who compete in them, only one person—only one—can hold the men's record, and only one person can hold the woman's record. So why is running marathons still such a popular sport? What is the possible appeal in a sport where 99.9 percent of all of the participants don't stand a chance of being first?

The answer: Marathons allow everyone to win!

Everyone entered may not be able to finish first, but everyone entered can still win. Marathons provide us with an opportunity to tap into man's oldest yardstick of accomplishment: simply being better than we've been in the past.

Marathon runners don't have to gauge their performance by anyone's standard but their own. Improving—even if it's by a second—is winning. In the New York Marathon, where the entrants each year number over 25,000, it is possible to have 25,000 winners. Think about that; 25,000 people can win!

Now, think about your business, your organization, or your family? Does it run like that? Do you have a scorekeeping and feedback system established in such a manner that maximizes the number of winners; that provides the majority of people in your organization with the opportunity to progress to succeed and, yes, even win? Does your organization have room for mass winning?

Coasters, Dodgers, Strivers & Waiters

We've talked a lot about the importance of distinguishing between mere measurement and productive, proactive scorekeeping. Nothing fits more clearly into the "mere measurement" category than the forced ranking systems that are so prevalent in American business. These are the statistical systems that rank workers, or players, according to an "average."

Essentially, it's the grading system from our school days, the hated bell curve, coming back to haunt us.

In school, you'll recall, a certain number of students get A's, another group gets B's, those in the "average" group get C's, and so on. Likewise, in business a certain number of workers are always going to be regarded as top, another group is going to be regarded as above-average, another group is going to be regarded as "average," and so on.

Most businesses, whether they know it or not, ascribe to the same rigid system as in school.

Instead of grades A, B, C, D, or F, I've given labels to these different groups that make up our business "curves." The superior group I refer to as "Coasters"—because that's the way they are perceived by the rest of the workers.

Coasters are those players the rest of the team sees as being in the best stores, the preferred locations. They're the ones who handle the reliable, established accounts; who have the boss's ear. These are the teacher's pets, grown up. Coasters are blessed and foreordained, in the view of those below them, to lives of favor and luxury that seem to have been mysteriously appointed them through no fault of their own. The group below them in hierarchy forgets the fact that when you see a person at the top of the mountain, it's a good bet that person didn't fall there.

Whether you call it jealousy or envy, the fact is that these Coasters, who are held up by management to be pillars of performance, are regarded by the rest of the troops as having reached some position unattainable by mere mortals. Those in the majority below will typically shift into survival mode and, just as the "A" students are left alone in school, the Coasters will be left alone in their penthouses. The unfortunate truth is that because of their position, these people have the greatest potential to improve their results. They need more coaching, not less.

The second group I call the "Dodgers."

In the tradition of the old trolley car dodgers in Brooklyn, these are the people who manage to keep one step out of harm's way by staying on the up side of the norm. They are "above average," and in business, as in school, that translates to being left alone. Management has better things to do, bigger fish to fry, more people to worry about and work with, than a Dodger.

The Dodgers realize this and are largely content in their anonymity. They don't want to go up, because they don't think they can; but they don't want to go down either, and they pray constantly that the Coasters above them won't really go to work and apply themselves because that would raise the average and threaten to knock the Dodgers out of their comfort zone.

The third group are the "Strivers," and they are the only people in the equation for whom the average has any real meaning.

Strivers are those workers whose performance falls close enough to the average line that they have a realistic shot at becoming Dodgers. So that is their goal: to get to the next level and become Dodgers themselves so they too can be left alone.

What the Strivers don't realize is that they are the ones who are responsible for raising the standard. The harder they work, the harder it gets. They're like the donkey chasing the stick on its back. The more they raise the average, the more difficult it is to attain it.

The fourth and final group are the "Waiters."

These are the people who have given up. They are waiting either for reassignment, a company remodel, or, eventually, retirement. They are convinced that the only difference between them and the Coasters is the territory they've been assigned, the stores they've been sent to, or, perhaps, a different alignment between Jupiter and Mars on the days that they decide to work. The Waiters are great at rationalization, and they'll typically rationalize themselves right into a stupor, becoming a liability to all but the curve, of which they are the downward anchor. Everyone above gives daily thanks for the Waiters.

Wherever "rankings" exist, there will always be Coasters, Dodgers, Strivers and Waiters. It is inevitable. And that means that, statistically speaking, 80 percent of those being ranked will be considered less than "winners" (think "A" students), and it is also guaranteed that there will be an equal number of "failures."

It's difficult to conceive of a system more counterproductive than a system that by definition relegates the vast majority of workers to positions that translate to "less-than-successful."

What is clearly needed is a way to get far more than 20 percent of the group to qualify as winners, and to do away entirely with the concept of failing "because somebody has to."

But you can't do that by encouraging everyone to become an "A" worker—a Coaster—because there simply isn't enough room. The math won't allow it. The curve will shut out the majority no matter what the standard.

The only way to do in the hated curve once and for all is to create scorecards that, like a marathoner's scorecard, are designed for the individual. Scorecards that will provoke a maximization of each individual's performance, whatever that might be. Scorecards that make it possible for everyone to win.

It is difficult to conceive of a system more counterproductive than one that by definition relegates the vast majority of workers to positions that translate to "less-than-successful."

Leveling the Playing Field

Anyone who plays golf knows it is a difficult game to control, let alone master. For most of us, shooting par is the impossible dream. Less than one percent of one percent (about one in a thousand) of those who play the game of golf are capable of scoring par or less for a regulation 18-hole round. Twenty-five percent of the people who play can't come within 25 percent of the stated goal of par.

Yet millions play golf every day in countries all around the world. People pay hundreds and thousands of dollars for the privilege. At the Pebble Beach Golf Links on the California coast, it costs $225 to play 18 holes—and you have to get in line for reservations. Each year billions are spent in America on golf equipment alone.

Why all the popularity for a game when almost no one can shoot par?

Because, as anyone who has gotten "hooked" by golf knows, you don't have to shoot par to win.

Despite its difficulty—and indeed, in many cases *because* of it—the scorecards and traditions of golf allow players to win on many levels.

For some people, breaking 100 might be the ultimate goal; for others, it might be breaking 90; still others, breaking 80.

Whatever it is, the very pursuit of that personal individual goal makes it possible for every golfer to win every time he or she tees it up.

Golf's simple scorekeeping system—basically one stroke for one swing of the club—makes it easy to know where we stand. We can constantly check whether we're winning or losing, in relation to our own goals and standards. It's an individual thing. The measurement isn't based on how everyone else performs, it's based on how each individual performs.

Even better, golf's scorekeeping system also employs a handicap system that allows greater clarification of where a player stands. This handicapping levels the playing field so that everyone, without regard to ability, can still "win."

In a simplified version, the handicap system works like this: after a player records a certain number of 18-hole scores, those scores are totaled and averaged. Then par is subtracted from that average score. The result creates a number that becomes that player's handicap. If a player's average score for 18 holes, for example, is 90, and par is 72, then that player's handicap will be 18—the result when you subtract 72 from 90. Again, this is the basic formula. It doesn't take into account the difficulty of the course, the throwing out of high scores, and other intricacies that go in to fine-tune golf's actual handicap system. But for our purposes here, this example will suffice.

Once golfers have their handicaps, they can then use them to gauge how close they are to par (the lower the handicap, the closer), and they can also use them when competing against players who also have handicaps, so that scores can be adjusted accordingly.

If your handicap is 18 and you play in a tournament and you score, say, 88, then your handicap-adjusted, or "net," score will be 88 minus 18, or 70. If you compete against a friend who has a handicap of 2 and he or she scores a 73, then his or her net score will be 73 minus 2—71. With your "handicap" you would be the victor in that match.

Now if you ask any golfer alive, they'll opt for a lower handicap, because a lower handicap translates to being a better golfer. No one's trying to pretend that the handicap system negates ability or the desire to improve. But what the handicap system does create is an environment where people with varying skills and abilities—and available practice time—can still compete, and it allows everyone to shoot par, relatively speaking.

The handicap system is a wonderful way of keeping score because it keeps everyone playing. It keeps everyone involved. No one is shut out. Everyone can "win." In terms of progress and the potential for satisfaction, the golfer who averages 90 has the same opportunity as the golfer who shoots 70.

The creators of the game of golf and its rules—and many other sports where handicap systems are also used, such as tennis and bowling—were astute enough to know that giving people handicaps increases participation, enthusiasm, and motivation. Without such a system, you shut out too many people from competing, and what's the sense of that? The reality is that few of us are at the Tiger Woods or Jack Nicklaus level, and never will be, no matter how hard we practice and no matter how much we would like to be. But a large percentage of us still want to compete. We want to be in the game. By applying handicaps to scorekeeping, varying levels of ability don't restrict participation, motivation, and striving toward goals.

It's naive to think that the workplace is any different. For a sales manager, for example, to think that all of his sales reps have the same capability and potential—that they can all excel at the level of the top producer—is no different than to think that all golfers can shoot par. In the human condition, it just ain't so. All golfers are not created equal. All sales reps are not created equal.

Wouldn't it be much more effective to allow each sales rep to work at reducing his or her own "handicap"—as established by properly designed scorecards—thereby clearing the way for everyone to compete on his or her own terms?

How much more conducive is it to personal development and overall improvement when players are given the freedom to not just know *how* to win, but to know they can *all* win?

> **F**or a sales manager to think that all the sales reps have the same capability and potential is no different than to think that all golfers can shoot par.

Make It Yours!

Our challenge here is to recognize and reward our below-average performer who delivers the largest increase in performance, even though he or she still does not reach above average. It is possible, but only when a system is in place that maximizes the number of winners.

Examples of some systems might include: scorecards on and recognition for largest percentage improvement over last year; largest dollar improvement in gross profit over previous period; largest sale of the year; largest increase in business from existing customer base; largest number of new accounts; greatest new account sales dollars. And the list goes on and on. Think of how short and uninspiring the Academy Awards would be if we only recognized Best Picture.

Resolve today to end ranking scorecards. Create instead, as one of our long-standing clients has done, a President's Club or an

Inner Circle or some other such honors group that justifies rewards. It is far better to have your sales force or individual crafts people have a noted recognition, a promotion to journeyman status, or an inner-circle acceptance which 50 percent or 60 percent, or 100 percent, of the sales force can accomplish. Maximizing the number of winners means maximizing the growth. Beginning today, modify your reward and recognition system to increase the number of winners next week, next month, and next year.

11

OWNERSHIP

Player buy-in makes all the difference.

Common Sense Coaching

everal years ago a large administration company that man-aged auto fleet programs for several of the largest corporations in America, with an inventory of over 100,000 cars, conducted a survey. Their research revealed that if companies wanted a sub-stantial (over 10 percent) reduction in maintenance and operating costs and a guarantee of a higher resale value on cars when they came back off lease, they should allow the user of the car to make one choice.

What was that choice? Was it the music system? Was it whether they got to keep the car or could buy it at the end? Was it the brand?

It was none of these.

The choice was color.

In fleets where drivers were allowed to pick the color of the car they drove, operating costs were substantially less than where car colors were randomly assigned, either by the fleet administrator, the purchasing department, or some other administrative entity.

When the car was the color of the driver's selection it magically became MY corporate car—and when the color was specified by the purchasing department or the fleet supervisor, it was THEIR company car.

Ownership has its benefits, and they are considerable.

You Gotta Go

There is a level of ownership that can only be described as "Gotta." Think of a movie that you have seen recently. One you enjoyed so much that after you saw it, you bought the video when it came out, and to all who would listen you simply said, "You *gotta* see it."

You gotta is more than a recommendation. It's more than an endorsement. It's a command for behavior. A command that conveys a propriety feeling; a sense of ownership.

When parabolic skis began to gain quick and ever-widening acceptance, the hot ski was a K2-4, with a pezo-electric vibration dampening technology. Nobody outside of the K2 design labs really knew what that meant, but thousands of skiers, many of them at the very best level of amateur skiing, after trying that ski would say to their friends, "You *gotta* get them, you *gotta* try them." The expression spoke for itself. It implied, "I've touched them," "I've played them," "I've tried them,"—and you've *gotta* try them too.

There is no limit to where this feeling of loyalty to something to which we have been truly converted can extend. It can translate to restaurants, to the kind of shoes we wear, to the pillows we sleep on, to a favorite kind of shampoo, to places to go on a vacation. Ask somebody who's been to the British Virgin Islands on a sailing trip. They'll say you *gotta* go to the Baths (a famous rock formation where huge boulders are piled up on the beach, providing a series of intricate and inviting tunnels and caverns). They'll probably add, "And you *gotta* eat at Foxy's on Jost Van Dyke."

It might be a particular shotgun or hand-tied graphite fly rod. It might be a boutique on Rodeo Drive. Or a junkstore disguised as an antique shop in Greenwich Village. But when people accept, embrace, and own something, either physically or psychologically, you can be sure that they will tell others, "You *gotta* do it baby."

This universal power and lure of ownership is something that can, and should, carry over into our scorekeeping. When there's a genuine feeling of ownership, a feeling that *this is valuable, and it belongs to me!*, the stage is then set for incredible buy-in, acceptance, and regular employment of the principles that are involved.

Tell Them Why, Not How

Whenever we ask people to execute or perform tasks, they're going to have three questions in mind:

- Why do you want it done?
- What do you want done?
- How do you want it done?

We get ownership of the task by the extent and the sequence in which we get answers to those questions. If I am your coach and we have no equity in our relationship and I'm asking you to do something you've never done before in your whole life, which one of those three questions are you going to want to have answered the most?

From the tens of thousands of people I've spoken to around the world, the answer is a resounding "I want to know why."

We want to know why first because the physiology of the relationship between the brain and the body says that until I determine why an action is necessary or required it's virtually impossible for me to do it. Anyone who has ever felt compelled or commanded to do a task without a legitimate reason knows how maddening that can be.

We also want to know why because it allows us to choose. Once we know *why*, we can then determine whether we are going to do it or not, how we are going to do it, when we are going to do it, and with whom.

When I tell you *why*, I communicate—in letters ten feet high— that you're important enough for me to tell why.

Now let's go back to our list of three questions. After the *"Why"* question, two are left: *"How"* and *"What."*

Which one of those questions do we like to have anwered the least?

Most of us would agree that we least like to be told *how*.

I hate to be told *how*. Why do I hate to be told *how*? I hate to be told *how* because it restricts my choices and therefore impedes my ownership. But primarily I hate to be told how because it says you think I'm stupid.

To important people we insist on explaining *why*, to unimportant people we simply tell *how*.

It's a fact that others can tell how we feel about them by the way we talk to them. By whether we tell them "why" or "how."

If we have ever gone in to borrow money or explained to a judge why the cop stopped us, we have experienced the innate desire to express why.

In fact, I'm sure some of us have prepared pages of whys, explanations and justifications, only to be cut off in mid-presentation by

The universal power and lure of ownership is something that can, and should, carry over into our scorekeeping.

a favorable result. We're now confronted with a conflict. We've gotten what we wanted, but we haven't had the opportunity to give all of our why's, and somehow we still feel frustrated.

Education psychologists report that the creativity peak in a person's life is reached at approximately age seven. If you interview second and third grade teachers and ask them what behavior changes as the child passes through that zenith of creativity, they will tell you the most observable behavioral change is that children stop asking *why*.

If we want to have a creative work force and we want to have a creative family or team of any nature, it's linked to continually telling why. When people are provided with "Why," they will own the choices that come as a result.

Competitive Forklifts

It follows that one important key to implementing scorecards is making sure that those who are going to be scored by them know why. To that end, we need to make sure that our scorecards reflect what coaches and players choose, instead of the result of arbitrary edicts from above.

This point was driven home to me when we implemented a GAME OF WORK scorekeeping system with a company that owned a huge warehouse measuring more than 1 million square feet.

One of this company's biggest challenges with implementing our scorekeeping system was to find a way to effectively keep score on the productivity of their letdown operator. That was their description for the forklift driver who circulates around the warehouse and moves pallets of merchandise from high storage slots down to eye-level locations so order selectors can see what they have to pick from and designate it for shipping.

Enthused by the prospect of creating his very own scorekeeping system, the warehouse manager announced, "I'm going to go out and rank all the letdown operators and create a competition among them."

Since it was, and still is, a long-held principle of THE GAME OF WORK that comparisons between participants should not be forced, but that the workers should be allowed to choose to compete, I strongly recommended that the manager modify his scorecards to better enable each forklift operator to compete within his own goals and expectations.

But when the manager came to our next session, his scorecards still measured the intra-company competition. They ranked the performance of the forklift operators from best to worst—in direct violation of our principles and my recommendation!

"Why did you do this?" I asked. "Why did you contradict everything we discussed?"

"It's what they wanted," he answered.

"Excuse me?" I asked.

"It's what they wanted," he replied again.

His point, and a good point it was, was that the men who operated the forklifts had determined among themselves that they would like to know how they stacked up against one another. *They* wanted the competition. While all my experience indicated that this would be counterproductive, the manager identified to me that there was a greater principle at work here—and that was the principle of *player buy-in*. Of ownership.

The best scorecard is the one the players want, the one they feel they own. That's the scorecard that's going to work!

The most powerful and useable scorecards are those that the players select and commit to by their own hand.

It turned out that the productivity of the letdown operators rose nearly 50 percent as a result of the new "competitive" scorecards. It was a group that, in this case, could not only handle the competition among themselves, but could thrive on it. This was particularly true because it was a competition they themselves had chosen and stamped with approval. They owned it.

A Chance to Change

Another fundamental advantage when it comes to this concept of ownership is the satisfying feeling generated when we say we "own" something. That gives us a sense of control. It frees us up to be proactive instead of reactive.

Here is a hypothetical example of what happens in far too many companies: Say I'm a sales manager at a store out "in the field," where I'm trying everything I can think of to help the business and make it successful. I dutifully send in my reports to corporate headquarters, where the accountants do my scores for me. Then they send the results to my boss. Because the boss gets the results before I do, I have no realistic opportunity to fix anything, to prepare myself for his or her reaction, even to perhaps steel myself against the criticism that might be coming.

> **T**he most powerful and useable scorecards are those that the players select and commit to by their own hand.

As a result, I don't feel like I have ownership in the scorekeeping, and I'm handcuffed. Instead of working in an atmosphere conducive to confidence and independent thinking, I work under a cloud of fear and a feeling that I'm not in control. Because I'm in no position to fix anything before I get in trouble for it, I'll naturally become defensive and guarded.

Conversely, if I get my score from accounting before the coach gets it—or, better yet, if I can compute it from effective scorecards that I can score myself—I'm going to have that important sense of ownership, and a much decreased frustration level.

Make It Yours!

Does your scorekeeping inspire the proprietory feelings that go hand-in-hand with ownership? Or does it generate the apathy generated by arbitrary and impersonal ways of measuring? It is far more important to have a system in place to which the players feel connected, however disjointed, than it is to have a system that might be efficient but out-of-touch and seen as the property of someone or something else. Ownership means loyalty and loyalty means a fierce desire to make it work. We believe in and take care of what we own.

What kind of pronouns does your team use? Do you hear, "I" "Me," "My," "Ours," and "We?" Or, do you hear, "You," "Yours," "They," "Them," "Those guys," and "Management?" Listen to what's being said. The personal pronouns selected by your team are the most reliable indicators of ownership. The power of personal choice generates ownership.

The Saturn car company, for example, has gone to great lengths to make its dealers understand and own the manufacturing process. The company encourages, and practically insists, on dealers visiting the manufacturing plant and the employees there, so that everyone feels like they are a part of the same team.

Allow your people to choose. Not just between two alternatives, or some alternate choice in a sales presentation. Not by hammering or bludgeoning. But by the very essence of true choice, by letting them have the opportunity to choose their methods. When they choose how to get a task done they can own what they are doing.

12

CREDIBILITY COUNTS

*The best scorecard is
the one you believe in.*

Common Sense Coaching

The inflation rate is something a lot of people talk about. And yet, how many of us know just exactly what the inflation rate is? Or, for that matter, how many of us know what makes up the Consumer Price Index, which is the primary factor in telling us the rate of inflation?

The truth is, not many. And even if we should go to the almanac and find that the Consumer Price Index, or CPI, is "a measure of the average change in prices over time of basic consumer goods and services," and, furthermore, that the CPI "is based on prices of food, clothing, shelter, fuels, transportion fares, charges for doctors' and dentists' services, drugs, and prices of the other goods and services bought for day-to-day living," we still are probably going to say, "Uh ... OK." Unless we take the time to study the formula calculated by the economists at the United States Department of Labor, most of us will still be inclined to take what the CPI says largely on trust.

But in spite of that, we'll still relate to it. We will because we accept it. We trust it. We know others trust it. Few of us could explain how the CPI is computed or swear under oath whether it's accurate or even if it relates to us. But we accept it because we see it as credible.

Earned Runs

For as long as anyone can remember, the preferred way to determine the value of a baseball pitcher is by a statistic called the Earned Run Average, which, essentially, is a ratio of earned runs (runs scored without the aid of fielding errors) allowed to innings pitched. An "ERA" is determined by dividing the number of innings a pitcher pitches by the number of "earned" runs he allows, and then multiplying by nine—the number of innings in a regulation game. In professional baseball, generally speaking, an ERA close to or below 3.00—meaning that the pitcher will, on average, allow three earned runs during a regulation game—is considered exceptional.

Starting from the lowest levels of organized baseball, pitchers know that their value will be calculated, to a large degree, according to their Earned Run Average. Players, fans, and coaches alike accept the ERA as a fair assessment of pitching ability. By the time a player gets to the big leagues, he knows and accepts the fact that his pay will be directly influenced by his ERA. In terms of today's huge salaries, the difference of just a single run in an ERA is going to translate into millions of dollars. A pitcher with a 2.90 ERA can command a $10 million yearly salary. A pitcher with a 3.90 maybe half that.

Yet, not only is no one quite sure of the origins of the Earned Run Average, but behind the scenes there is an ongoing debate as to its fairness.

In the book, *Baseball by the Numbers*, baseball analyst Willie Runquist writes, "Neither runs nor earned runs are a realistic assessment of pitching performance ... the definition of *earned run* more than occasionally fails to capture the reality of the pitching peformance."

Runquist goes on to explain that the problems with the Earned Run Average are in the definition of *innings pitched* and other intricacies we don't need to go into for our purposes here. But what's interesting to me—a student of scorekeeping—is the conclusion Mr. Runquist makes after taking apart the Earned Run Average, exposing all its flaws, and pretty much destroying its capacity for fairness.

"This does not mean," he writes, "that the Earned Run Average is not a useful statistic. It has proven its viability over the years."

Just how has it "proven its viability?" By the unbelievable "credibility" given it by the players involved, that's how. The simple truth is, the Earned Run Average works because everyone agrees it works.

Make It Relevant

A key component for effective scorekeeping is player acceptance and enthusiasm, as widespread acceptance of the Earned Run Average suggests. Credibility counts more than either accuracy or understanding. The best-planned, most well-thought-out scorecard on earth will do little or no good without player sanction and acceptance.

I saw that firsthand when THE GAME OF WORK was called in to a large bottling plant that, in spite of implementing a meticulous measuring system, was having tremendous problems increasing bottle-line productivity. No matter how hard they tried, they were unable to increase the number of bottles and cases they were producing per hour, day, week, and so on.

The measuring system they were using assessed productivity according to what this company called Utilization. Management had brought in an industrial engineer to devise utilization, and it was truly a sight to behold. Imagine the Earned Run Average on steroids. The Utilization measurement was thought out to the smallest decimal point. The idea was to chart how much an employee *utilized* the assets he or she was given stewardship over. The extremely complex formula was driven by flow meters, benchmarking, target rates, and a number of other statistics inherent to the beverage industry. Utilization was a beautiful thing in the eye of the engineer who created it.

In the eyes of the players whose performance it monitored, however, utilization was a repressive, negative nightmare. They did not understand it, they did not know how to calculate it. But worst of all, they did not see it as relevant.

Now, lack of understanding wasn't that critical. As we've already discussed with the Consumer Price Index and Earned Run Average examples, neither an intricate knowledge of the formula nor a perfect formula are necessary for effective, highly motivating scorekeeping. Quite often, being complex doesn't matter either.

But relevance IS important. Because relevance bestows credibility.

And credibility to the player is imperative!

If the players inherently realize that the system, its quirks notwithstanding, still manages to accurately reflect what's going on, they'll buy the system hook, sinker, and bottom line.

In the bottling plant, utilization just wasn't getting the job done.

When we substituted the engineer's high-priced system of measurement with scorecards that simply looked at units of production in terms of cases or cans per labor hour, not only did we see an almost immediate improvement in the number of cases and cans per hour but magically, for the first time in years, the company was able to produce an improvement in—you guessed it—utilization. By operating with a scorekeeping system the players bought into, the players accomplished what management was after in the first place!

The important point is when you are faced with the choices of a scorecard approved by industrial engineering or finance or any of the management sciences, and a scorecard designed by, and for, the players in the game, it is always better to do it pretty much the way the players want it. *There is a tremendous difference between a plan designed **by you** for you to use and a plan designed **by us** for you to use.*

There is a tremendous difference between a plan designed *by you* for you to use and a plan designed *by us* for you to use.

Appeal Is Everything

Recently, one of our clients provided an excellent, as well as humbling, example to me of the importance of the concept of player buy-in and credibility.

After an initial GAME OF WORK seminar presentation to a large supermarket chain in the Northeast, the company decided it wanted to keep score on what is called "shrink."

Now "shrink," for those uneducated in the supermarket jargon, is the term used to refer to "We-don't-know-where-it-went-money." Supermarkets don't use "We-don't-know-where-it-went-money" because it's too long, and also because bankers probably wouldn't be too excited about the term. So they use "shrink." But that's what it is—money that slips through the cracks due to a variety of things, including product spoilage, employee theft, customer theft, inventory errors, and damaged product. The accumulated bottom line, or shrink, accounts for money that just disappeared.

Shrink is a big deal. In most supermarket businesses, it's equal to, and in some cases greater than, the total net profit. It's a huge number in that industry.

This particular supermarket chain deduced that if it could significantly reduce shrink, there would be an immediate impact on profitability. They set out to do something about it by setting up scorecards to measure shrink per labor hour, i.e. the percentage of the total shrink attributable to each hour of labor worked.

Now if you're saying to yourself, "Man, that must have been

hard to get a handle on!", you're thinking the same thing I thought. I thought this was the craziest sounding scorecard I'd heard of in my life. Since shrink, by definition, is largely a mystery anyway, there was simply no way to find all the shrink. It was anybody's guess, going in, just how much they'd be able to track at all with this formula. All my consulting instincts said we were going down the wrong track. I said to myself, this is nuts, it's a goofy scorecard, it makes no sense. Ain't going to work.

But they were insistent, and even more significant, they were enthusiastic, and since a key component of THE GAME OF WORK is allowing the players to decide what's important to give feedback on, and therefore important to score, I kept my fears to myself, consoled by the thought that trial and error can be a good thing in the search for truly effective scorecards.

I was sure they'd fail.

To put some shape on their elusive shrink, they limited their scorekeeping to what is known as visible shrink—that's the term for products that have gone stale, are out of code, have been broken on the shelf, or have been stolen. Enthusiastically embracing scorekeeping and THE GAME OF WORK, they set about tracking this visible shrink.

It would be just a matter of time I thought, before they would change their parameters, and their scorecards. I expected they'd find little or no relationship between charting this visible shrink and profitability.

But after a month the operating statements came back and, based on the company's new scorekeeping, shrink had shrunk— and net profit had grown.

Their scorecards were working.

I was glad I'd kept my mouth shut.

Still, I suspected it might just be beginner's luck. Because of all the unknowns involved, I wasn't sure about the endurability of their scorecard. I wasn't convinced it would last.

But another month went by and shrink had shrunk again, and profitability continued to rise. The third month, same thing, and the fourth month, and so on.

The wonderful thing about the process, I was forced to conclude, was that what really happened was the increase in awareness of the problem caused behavior to change. The shrink was reduced because of what the players chose to do as a result of that increased awareness: better surveillance of shoplifters, taking better care of product so spoilage was cut to a minimum, and so on.

In reality, the players couldn't really do anything about the actual shrink, because no matter how you define it, shrink is an unknown. Nonetheless, they had taken a measurement that had never been used before in the industry and used it to create a scorecard that was enthusiastically bought by the players. So what if it was a number with no real backing or basis? So what if you took their numbers to the American Institute of Certified Public Accountants. Not only would they not certify them, they would probably make you certifiable!

No matter. The important thing was that it made sense to the players. They felt they had influence. They felt they had the capacity for real change. And since that's what they honestly felt, that made all the difference.

Make It Yours!

Resolve today. Begin now that when faced with a difference of opinion or a conflict between the way your people want to do it, the way you think it ought to be done, the way headquarters wants it done, or to compromise—do it *exactly* the way your people want to do it. We have asked far too many, for far too long, to change too much, to satisfy too few who were too far from the action. We frankly, from a corporate America standpoint, ask people who are responsible for serving our customers, meeting them, feeding them, and touching them, to jump through unbelievable and incredible hoops. So when people say to you how do you feel about this business and you ask is this scorekeeping system credible, too many times they'll say, oh no, this is incredible.

So begin today, resolve today, continue today, to give workers the opportunity and the capacity to grow by doing what is credible to them. If they want to measure pounds and purchasing wants to measure percentages, let's measure pounds. The point is that they will tell you what's credible. They will become more productive because of their ownership in a scorekeeping system that they created and they believe to be credible.

13

WE TRUST WHAT
WE CAN TOUCH

*The best scorekeeping is
self-administered.*

Common Sense Coaching

our guys are playing golf. They finish the first hole. One has made a birdie, one a par, and two have made bogeys. As they walk from the green they look at each other, wondering who has the scorecard. It turns out no one has it. They each forgot to get a scorecard before they started. What, then, is the appropriate behavior in this situation? The appropriate behavior is the 900-yard golfer dash—450 yards to the starter's shack, 450 yards back to the second tee. Because nobody is going to play without the scorecard.

People trust what they can touch; what they can see. They like it best when they keep and monitor their own score.

Hands-on

I was at a Senior PGA Tour event a few years ago when I walked past a tent set up next to the 18th green. Three men sat inside on folding chairs.

"What's that, and who are they?" I asked the official I was with.

"Scoring tent. Scorers," came the reply.

There were 144 players that day in the Pro-Am tournament, and these three guys, sitting in the tent, not watching a single shot, were able to accurately keep track of the whole thing!

Why was this possible? It was possible because in golf, the scorecard is close to the players. They keep their own score. All the guys in the scoring tent had to do was take the information relayed to them from the players on the course and reproduce it on the overall scorecard.

Such a format is not unique to golf. Most games have self-administered scorekeeping. A lot of cities have large-scale, family-type tennis tournaments, for example. These tournaments can be "run" by very few official scorekeepers because in all the matches, the scores are kept by the participants. Everyone knows how to keep score and there's a built-in trust factor and honor code involved that keeps everything honest. The system works because the players make it work.

People trust what they can touch.

Keeping Track

One day the phone rang in our offices at THE GAME OF WORK. Two partners of a major electrical supply firm were on the other end, inquiring about our services. Their opening line was succinct and to the point. "Sales are going to hell in a handbasket," they said. "We need help!"

In our first meeting, the partners called in their corporate sales manager, a man making well into six figures, to join us. I got right to the point.

"Is the problem smaller orders or fewer orders?" I asked, looking at the sales manager.

The sales manager looked dumbfounded.

Again I asked, "Which is it—smaller orders or fewer orders?"

The sales manager looked at the partners, who were looking at each other, and then back at the sales manager, who finally broke the silence by declaring, "I don't know."

After another long pause, someone said, "I think Diane knows."

Now we were making some headway. "Who's Diane?" I asked. "She's the one who does entry," I was told. Moments later we found Diane at her desk in the main office, dutifully working away.

Taking the lead, the sales manager looked at Diane and pointed to the computer on the desk in front of her. "Diane," he asked, "will that thing tell us how many orders we have each day?"

"Sure won't," answered Diane, who, it turned out, had a delightful sense of timing.

After letting just enough time lapse, with the three biggest bosses in the company in front of her, she finally added, "Would you like to know?"

"I thought that thing wouldn't tell us," the sales manager responded.

"It won't," said Diane, who, after another well-timed pause, asked, "Would you like to know?"

I began to understand that Diane wanted to tell us something.

"Diane," I said, "I would really like to know."

"OK," she said, and then, from just underneath that IBM 3800 or whatever it was that they probably rented for three or four thousand a month, she opened a little desk drawer on the work table in front of her and pulled out a calendar. It was just a simple calendar, the kind that vendors give out every Christmas, with squares for each day. In each business day she had used her pencil to make marks, tick, tick, tick, tick, cross; tick, tick, tick, tick, cross, and so on. There were marks for every day. I was amazed. Day-in, day-out, Diane had tracked the business's sales orders.

The sales manager said, "Diane, who told you to do that?"—as if original thought were against company policy.

She looked up at him and said, "Nobody."

I jumped in again. "Diane, why do you do that?"

She looked at me with an innocence that was wonderful and unforgettable. "Oh," she answered, "it just makes me feel better when we do more than 200 orders a day."

The manager with a six-digit income didn't have a clue, but Diane just felt better when they did 200 orders a day!

The reality is that scorekeeping is such a powerful and natural motivator that people do it when they aren't even asked.

I said, "Diane, may I borrow that?" She said "Sure." I scooped up the calendar and as the sales manager and I walked out of the office, Diane asked, again with perfect timing, "Would you like last year's?"

From day one, it turned out, Diane had been doing the tracking.

From Diane's information we were able to determine that, in fact, the number of orders being taken by the company was as strong as it had ever been. But the size of the orders, we subsequently discovered, was down by 14 percent.

With that information, we were then able to design scorecards that concentrated on order size, not frequency. In three and a half days, the sales force succeeded in beefing up the size of its orders to levels near the old figures. From there, continuous growth was not far away. Today, that organization is a leader in its industry.

In another example, we saw a produce department manager at a grocery store get in touch with the business by physically counting the cases of produce in stock when each new truck arrived with a fresh delivery. The process did not require a computer, or corporate accounting, it didn't even require much math. But he had nonetheless established a touchable scorecard which he believed in; and if he could improve the numbers on that scorecard, i.e., reduce the number of cases remaining when the new shipments arrived, he could predict improvement in the overall financial scorecard for the company.

He was right.

Within the very first accounting period, he could see a direct correlation between improvements in his "touchable" scorecard and the profitability report that came down from corporate headquarters.

> **The reality is that scorekeeping is such a powerful and natural motivator that people do it when they aren't even asked.**

Make It Yours!

You managers out there reading this, take note. Look for the closet scorekeepers. Instead of wanting to string up the person who takes charge of the office football pool, find out how to tie in that motivation for scorekeeping and feedback and apply it to what you pay that person for. Take advantage of that natural force, the urge we all have to know how we're doing, to know what the score is. If we can just create the right environment, people will bury us with their enthusiasm. Scorekeeping is merely a vehicle for us to get feedback. Look for the key people and start keeping score.

14

A BETTER WAY

*There is always plenty of room
for improvement.*

Common Sense Coaching

When my grandfather ran his grocery store, he didn't have an electronic cash register. He had a manual register that showed the customer how much the sale was, but there was no accumulator, no running total. So my grandfather's accountant said to him, "Why don't you give everybody a hand-written sheet when they make purchases, keep a copy for yourself, throw your slips in the drawer, and I'll come by once a month and add them up?"

So that's what my grandfather did. That's the premise that monthly profit-and-loss statements are based on. But today, we have electric cash registers, not to mention scanners, computer programs, and many other technological advantages that give us the ability to instantly record transactions. Yet, too many businesses are still throwing the slips in the shoebox in the drawer, waiting until the accountant comes by and does the month-end.

Scorekeeping Lags Behind

Many of the measurements that we have today came to us as a result of what was done long ago. We are surrounded by the ultra-modern. We work in buildings that are perfectly climate controlled. On state-of-the-art photocopiers we make copies Rembrandt would have been proud to call his own. We heat gourmet meals in the microwave. We conference call on cell phones and check out the latest market updates instantaneously on the Internet. Yet we "keep score" like we always have. We get in a measuring groove and we stay there.

They don't do this in games. In games they're always tinkering with the scorekeeping to increase interest, enthusiasm, and motivation, and to improve the game.

When Dr. James Naismith first invented what he called "basket ball," he hung two peach baskets on the opposite ends of the YMCA gymnasium in Springfield, Mass. and didn't remove the bottoms of the baskets. Whenever a player made a "basket," someone would record the score, and then someone else, who was standing on the balcony above the gym, would reach in the peach basket, remove the ball, and toss it back to the court. In gymnasiums where balconies didn't exist, they'd put up ladders next to the baskets. Every time the ball went in the basket, they'd count the "basket," and then someone would climb up the ladder and retrieve the ball.

But then came that great moment in the history of basketball when someone cut the bottom out of the basket.

Now the ball could drop straight through, right back into the hands of the players. It wasn't long before they decided to not stop play any more after each basket. Suddenly, basketball became a game of action. There was less standing around. Less waiting. Scoring shot up. Cutting the bottom out of the basket was a simple improvement, but very significant nonetheless.

Basketball didn't stop there. They've been tinkering with the game ever since. They outlawed goaltending one year, they painted in the 10-second midcourt line another year, and painted in the keyhole after that. Now there's a time clock and even the standard two-points-per-basket rule was not inviolate. Now longer shots are given three points. If Dr. Naismith were to see the game he invented today, he would barely recognize it.

What if businesses adopted that kind of introspection and change? Are there peach baskets just waiting to have their bottoms cut out in your business?

Then came the great moment in the history of basketball when someone cut the bottom out of the peach basket. Are there peach baskets in your business waiting to have their bottoms cut out?

Catching Up

One of the oldest sports in the world is archery. There are pictures of archers on caves dating back thousands of years. In Greek mythology, Apollo was an archer. As a competitive sport, the international archery association, the Federation de Tir a l'Arc (FITA), has been around since 1931, and archery has been an Olympic sport since the 1972 Games in Munich.

But in spite of its rich heritage, long history and many traditions, interest in Olympic archery was so ambivalent that by the 1980s the International Olympic Committee recommended dropping the sport from the Games.

So what did archery do in response? Throw a fit because some-one was challenging its tradition? Refuse to change? Nope. FITA changed the way it keeps score. Instead of having every competitor shoot hundreds of arrows at four different distances and then adding up the points, as was done in the past, a much faster-paced "Olympic elimination round" was instigated. This new plan called for the archers to pair off in arrow-for-arrow showdowns, with run-ning scores kept after each shot on a huge electronic scoreboard. Suddenly, archery was easy to follow.

Just like that, interest in archery picked up and the sport's Olympic demise was averted.

Archery is just one example to show how games routinely respond to the times and adjust and upgrade the way they operate and the way they keep score. Look at what they did in golf. For years, ties at the end of golf's "major" tournaments—the United States and British Opens, the Masters, and the PGA Championship—were decided by 18-hole rounds that would be played the following day.

But when interest in these rather laborious tie-breakers dropped off, three of the four tournaments changed their formats to some form of sudden death play-off immediately following the final round. Only the U.S. Open held firm. It's interesting to note the increased interest and attendances in the three majors that responded to the times and changed, and the criticisms that con-tinue to be leveled at the U.S. Golf Association for refusing to budge.

The examples go on and on. In most NBA basketball arenas, as well as many college arenas, you can now see the stats for every player on the giant electronic scoreboards—and not just rebounds and points anymore, but other statistics such as steals, assists, fouls, etc. Ten years ago, the scoreboards weren't nearly as elaborate. The constant improvements reflect an increasing awareness of the value of scoreboard awareness.

Scoreboards and scorekeeping can always be improved and updated.

Changing Times

Around the time of World War II, the cash register made its appearance on the business stage, and a significant appearance it was. With cash registers in place in supermarkets, for example, the stores could generate accurate information about purchases in var-ious departments. There was a key for meat, a key for grocery, a key for bakery goods, and so on.

107

It was a huge breakthrough because now the individual department managers could actually tell how sales in their separate areas were doing.

But the thing is, here it is 50 years later, and what do you think most stores are still using for their measurement? That's right. The cash register. The invention from half a century ago remains the most often utilized scorecard among American supermarkets to give an indication of how well the individual department is doing.

This is true in spite of the fact that since the mid-1970s most supermarkets, thanks to the invention of computer scanners, have had the capacity to refine and improve their measuring with a much more detailed system. It's called customer penetration. The computer drives it with the scanning code, which provides information by department, by item, and so forth.

Instead of merely reporting volume, scanners report the average purchase per customer in the department itself and the percentage of total store customers who in fact make a purchase in each individual department.

The data from this new way of looking at the business allows managers to take a far deeper look into what's going on. It affords them the capability to look at department business sales in the two key component parts—A) Traffic, and B) How well we're doing with the people once we get them there. Plus, it allows managers to more effectively respond because they have better diagnostics of what behavior stands between them and the goals they want to accomplish.

But in spite of the obvious benefits, few stores today routinely give their managers feedback on this important level of performance. Hamstrung by tradition, they continue to operate with a system that is far less effective. The cash register.

What makes this doubly disconcerting is that supermarkets have actually built a business selling this same scanner-produced data to grocery manufacturers who then use it to sell more product to the stores. So the grocery people are actually making it available to the manufacturers so they can do a better job of selling them product, but they don't use it to do a better job of selling *their* own customers more product.

The reality is that by giving the department managers their percentage of total store customers, the supermarkets could enable the managers to set concrete goals for realistic and attainable performance. This, in turn, would create the opportunity for all managers to win each week—as opposed to traditional measuring systems which demand, by virtue of their mathematical certainty, that for every successful manager we will have one manager who will be unsuccessful.

Historically, managers have been judged according to the percentage of the total they produced. Which means that every time the produce department gets more business, the non-foods or bakery has to give up some business.

Only when we take advantage of the new scorekeeping technology and say we're going to take a look at and track the percentage of the customers who come in the department and make a purchase from us, do we put ourselves in a situation where we have a better opportunity to get the customer to make a complete shopping pass in the store—and everybody has a much greater chance of being successful.

Turn & Don't Earn

Equally as important as changing with the times is examining systems of measurement that, despite being in place for as long as anyone can remember, may in fact be encouraging a lack of performance because of the potential for misreadings and misconceptions.

As an example, there is an age-old business measurement concept called Turn & Earn. Basically the formula counts the number of turns in an inventory times the gross profit percentage. So theoretically, if I'm turning an inventory 15 times a year and I calculate my percentage profit margin in it, I'll come up with a whole number that represents my Turn & Earn measurement.

For years, many in industry have maintained that this is a good combination scorecard, purported to be a great way to evaluate the folks in purchasing. If the Turn & Earn number increases, reflecting more turns and more gross margin, or earnings, that means purchasing is doing a better job. If the turn and earn number decreases, just the opposite is believed to be true.

But look what happened a couple of years ago in the paper business—one that typically employs the use of Turn & Earn. There was a serious paper shortage, industry-wide, that resulted in high demand and short supply. As a result, prices predictably rose. That in turn resulted in percentage profit margins that were up to 50 percent higher than traditional.

Translation: If I'm in purchasing and I want to maintain my usual Turn & Earn "score," I only have to work half as hard as in the past. I can turn half as much as before and still get the same score I was getting before the shortage hit.

This is a good example of a bad scorecard. Instead of getting a real sense of control, the people in purchasing let the inventory turns erode substantially because they could produce higher margins regardless. As you can imagine, such behavior resulted in considerably less productivity.

In order to be effective, the Turn & Earn scorecard needed to be tweaked to include safeguards against variables when times were not "normal."

Make It Yours!

If you want to build player enthusiasm, player motivation, and player performance where you work, you need a scorekeeping system that is dynamic and *current*. You need one that reveals pertinent information that will motivate and increase productivity, not simply satisfy a need for corporate accounting.

The questions you want to ask in your businesses are these: "Is there a better way to do this?" "Is there a better way to keep score?"

Just because it hasn't been done before doesn't mean it can't be done now.

Just because there's never been a scorecard in the form of some kind of base test for the keyboard operators, for example, why couldn't there be? Why shouldn't keyboard operators have their own scorecards to look at, their own targets to shoot at, their own marathons to run? Why shouldn't checkers at the supermarket have their own scorecards? Why shouldn't forklift operators and truck drivers and secretaries and CEOs and COOs and CFOs? Why shouldn't every employee, and every manager, in every business, whatever their task?

If you have a scorekeeping system currently in place and if it is motivating everyone involved, if it's accentuating the positive, then fine. If it's not, then it's time to make changes and improve.

The Concepts of Scorekeeping

15

KEEP IT SIMPLE

When in doubt, simplify.

Common Sense Coaching

The great general Napoleon Bonaparte was reputed to have had a full-ranking general on his staff with an I.Q. of less than 100. People asked the general, "What is the man's purpose?" and "Why would you have him if he's such a fool?"

"He's my communications specialist," was Napoleon's reputed answer. "I send written orders to him and ask him to tell me what they mean. I rewrite orders and rewrite them until I have at least a 90 percent agreement from him on my meaning. When I do that, I know I have at least a 70 percent chance of my genius generals understanding my meaning."

What Napoleon understood is that the brilliance of an order is not determined by its flowery vocabulary as much as it is dictated and driven by the effectiveness of that order to link up with your listener's ability to understand and relate.

The Big Board

One of the big success stories in charity fund-raising is the major impact caused by telethons—those marathon entertainment programs that solicit donations to the television station. The universal centerpiece for these telethons has become a large scoreboard that clearly shows both the current tally and the hoped-for grand total. Usually there's another figure that shows how far the two are apart.

The numbers on these scoreboards are always readibly visible. No one is left to guess how much money has been raised and how close, or far away, the goal still is. The reason these "big boards" have become so popular is because they work. People respond to the simple feedback constantly delivered by a simple scoreboard. It doesn't have to be very clever, very cute, or very complex. Nor does it have to be generated by complicated demographic studies, excessive graphics, and a lot of audience data. Just so it says how much we've raised, and how much we want to raise. That's enough for Jerry's Kids, and it's enough for any business, too. The issue here is simplicity—and how well it works.

In his tape on strategies, Vic Braden, the great tennis instructor, says that their survey indicates that at the championship tennis level, finalists go into their matches with two strategies at the most. In club championships, people typically go into their matches with four or five strategies. C level players in most tennis clubs have 20 or 30 strategies. No strokes, just strategies. It has been said that being a professional is the art of taking the difficult and making it look easy. One way to do that is to make sure that you and your team are focused on the basics.

Another example of this can be found with a review of Super Bowl champions. The most predictable statistic in the Super Bowl is that the team that rushes for the most yards wins the ball game. Not the team with the fanciest pass plays, or the trickiest formations, but the one that is successful at simply moving the football on the ground.

Bag Control

We were doing work with a large grocery store chain in Southern California that was having trouble managing bagging expense. Now bagging expense—the amount used for the plastic and paper bags customers carry their groceries in—is not inconsequential in the supermarket industry. It will typically run 15 to 25 percent of net operating income in a store that's making money, and much more than that in one that's not making money. It is a big deal in the business, and controlling it is a constant challenge for management.

This particular chain's approach to controlling bagging expense was to periodically call their people together, rant and rave about the expense being too high, and demand for a stop to double-bagging, wasting, giving away bags, and so on. There was really no mechanism for feedback in place, just good old-fashioned lecturing.

Bag expense would usually be better for a month or two after these tirades, but then it would increase and management would again resort to yelling, cajoling, and threatening. The vicious cycle wasn't much fun for anyone involved, not for management, and certainly not for the baggers.

During our GAME OF WORK implemention we suggested that if baggers could know on a weekly basis how effectively they were using the bags, that could greatly influence in their behavior. They needed their own scorecard, in other words. They needed to be able to tell.

To keep this weekly score, we selected a computation of bags used per customer. Was it simple? Absolutely. Was there a potential for a lot of variations? Yes. But the stores decided it was worth a try.

The logistics for our scorekeeping simply amounted to counting the number of bags each week and relating that to the number of customers. The closer the number of bags to number of customers, the better. It would take less than 15 minutes a day to compute. To ensure player visibility, these scorecards were posted near the time clock.

The improvement was immediate, and it only got better. Just one month under this system of scorekeeping, an entire railroad car of grocery bags, ordered on an automatic order program, arrived at the warehouse with no place to be stored because of the effectiveness of the program. In a little less than 90 days, this company found itself on a steady run rate that would ultimately result in $600,000 every year in reduced expense and increased profitability.

The only thing in it for the baggers was recognition and a sense of enjoyment that they were participating in something meaningful and productive. That was enough. The reality was that if they did a good job yesterday, they would come to work and get feedback on the good job they did, as opposed to the old way, which amounted to being recognized (yelled at) only when they messed up, and only on a quarterly basis. Just by knowing each day how they were doing—the result of a simple scorecard anyone could have created—the baggers were able to feel good about their contribution, and, in the bargain, save the company a considerable expense.

When there's a choice between something simple and straightforward, and something with a lot of working parts, which no one understands, the simple and straightforward is going to win out.

Cardboard Alternative

Usually, when there's a choice between something simple and straightforward and something with a lot of working parts, which no one understands, the simple and straightforward is going to win out.

A large soft drink bottling plant found this out. Management installed an expensive piece of measuring equipment (the price tag was $65,000) with the grand scheme that it would take the plant to

115

a new height of 1,100 cases per labor hour. This sophisticated system was designed to track all kinds of data that would allow the workers on the line to keep the operation running at its greatest capacity.

But once the equipment was in place, the only part of it the workers immediately took to was the clock. The employees used it to know when it was time to go on break.

At this juncture, a man named Cyril Chong entered the scene. Cyril had just gone through our GAME OF WORK program and he returned to the plant with the importance of player feedback and simplicity keen on his mind. Anxious that the plant would have frequent and effective feedback, Cyril took it upon himself to physically measure the number of cases they were running through the system every hour and writing that number down on the back of one of the large cardboard boxes that hold 24 cans of pop. Since it was very noisy while the plant was operational, Cyril would simply hold up his cardboard box every hour so the workers on the shift could see, in big, bold, black letters, how they were doing.

As Cyril continued to do that, productivity began to rise, first from 675 to 750 cases per man-hour, then to 825, to 900, and finally to the 1,100 cases that everyone had previously thought would only be possible by utilizing the expensive piece of measuring equipment that lay dormant in the plant ... except for the clock.

The February 1918 *Success* magazine described how U.S. Steel chairman Charles Schwab helped a mill manager find a new way to motivate his workmen. "Schwab asked a man from the day shift how many heats they had made that day. 'Six, sir' was the reply. Getting a piece of chalk, Schwab chalked a big '6' on the floor.

"When the night shift arrived, they were curious what the '6' meant and were duly informed. The next morning, Schwab saw a bigger '7' in place of the '6'. On his next visit, the '7' was gone, replaced by a big '10.' The mill, which had been the poorest producer in the plant, became chief producer."

Make It Yours!

We've all heard the K.I.S.S. formula and historically it means "Keep It Simple Stupid." I would like to modify that acronym and, while maintaining its intent, put it in a more positive vein:

Keep It Solidly Simple.

Keep your scorekeeping solidly simple. Read it and re-read it, simplify it and simplify it again, until you're satisfied it is in a form easily understood, and embraced, by all who will use it for direction and motivation.

You can try this simplicity test. Pretend that your board of directors is made up of third graders. Now cut through all the hyperbole of your annual report and determine how you would tell them in fifteen minutes the nature of your business.

"It doesn't mean anything; but for some reason, it just makes me feel good!"

16

CONTROL–
INFLUENCE–
IMPACT

You don't need absolute control
in order to have influence and impact.

Common Sense Coaching

Most people will say they're only willing to measure or keep score on or be held accountable for that which they can control. This is a fallacy. The reality is that the people who get rewarded only for what they can directly control don't get much of a reward.

The truth is, in business, and in life, we often have very little control at all. It's what we influence that really matters. CEOs of Fortune 500 companies actually control a very small amount of what is going on in their companies, and they certainly cannot directly control the attitudes, motivation, desires and goals of thousands of people in their employ. Most of us can't control the market place or the competition we are linked to. Whether we win or lose is based much more upon what we can influence and have an impact on, than it is upon what we can directly control.

Life Story

It was the late great baseball manager Casey Stengel who used to say that the secret to managing a ball club is keeping the half who don't like you away from the half who haven't made up their mind.

Now that may not be the most preferred methodology of any current managerial guidebooks, but there's a point in what ol' Casey had to say. Managing is a lot less about control than it is about maneuvering. On a baseball team it's an easy principle to see. The manager of the team can't really control his players in the strict sense of the word. He can't get them to hit or run or slide or bunt if they don't want to. He can't do it for them or make them do it. He doesn't have that kind of control.

But he can, by giving his players pertinent information, guide them where he wants them to go and give them every good reason why they should want to go there themselves.

Control is overrated. Influence, and the impact that results from postitive influence, is vastly underrated.

Consider the example of one of the biggest success stories in American business in the last twenty years—the National Basketball Association.

Control is overrated. Influence, and the impact that results from positive influence, is vastly under-rated.

There was a time, and it wasn't that long ago, that basketball ran a distant third in popularity when it came to professional sports in America. Baseball and football were much bigger in terms of fan followings, player salaries, ticket prices, television contracts, and so on. Cities waited in line to acquire major league baseball or National Football League franchises.

But today, basketball is most definitely on a par with football and baseball. In some areas, particularly the international arena, basketball is ahead of both of them.

Most analysts agree that it's no coincidence that the beginning of the NBA's resurgence dates back to the early 1980s when a New York City lawyer named David Stern took over as league commissioner. Under Stern's leadership, NBA franchise values have increased many times over, attendance has skyrocketed, the league's TV contract package is one of the most lucrative in sports, the players' salaries are ten times what they were two decades ago, and even the referees' salaries are miles beyond where they once were.

The remarkable thing about all this progress is that individual franchises in the NBA are all run as private enterprises. Like all the commissioners who came before him, David Stern came into his position as a counselor and adviser, nothing more. He had no real power. The commissioner doesn't own anything. He can't tell anyone what to do.

As commissioner, Stern could only counsel and advise. So that's what he's done. David Stern merely showed the franchises how it would work to all of their advantage if they did some things together. If they practiced revenue sharing in some key areas such as merchandising and national TV rights, for example, and if they collectively agreed on a salary cap to keep personnel costs manageable. His advice was that they would all be better off, including the players. In other key areas, such as expansion and aggressive international marketing, Stern has been able to convince the individual franchise owners to proceed in a similar cooperative fashion. All this in spite of the commissioner's limited powers.

The result has been uncommon harmony and prosperity in a very turbulent industry.

120

Brokers

Consider the case of real estate brokers. A successful real estate broker is going to be compensated based on how well he or she influences the behavior of independent sales agents over whom he or she has no direct control. As a matter of fact, as far as the Internal Revenue Service is concerned, to qualify for special tax status an independent agent by definition is one who cannot be controlled by the broker, or anyone else, for that matter.

Nonetheless, any successful real estate broker knows that helping independent agents identify where their income is coming from and how effectively and efficiently they are running their autonomous enterprise is the cornerstone for boosting agent productivity and, when necessary, facilitating a change in agent behavior.

The astute broker uses whatever is at his or her disposal to illuminate just how these independent agents are doing. Controlling may be officially taboo, but influence—and impact—know no boundaries.

A good scorekeeping system is, of course, the key to providing an all-encompassing look at an agent's activities.

This point was well made a few years ago with a large real estate brokerage that serviced independent agents across the country. The company had been founded on a single principle, one it strictly adhered to, that said that aggressive local classified newspaper advertising is the key to a successful real estate operation. The company held an underlying corporate belief which said that ads placed in such a manner brought in a majority of a realtor's business.

The franchises followed this belief loyally, and also blindly. Because the truth was, while on paper the classified ad theory seemed to make sense, in reality it didn't work all that well. This "fact" was uncovered by a secretary in the home office who took it upon herself to apply a scorecard to the brokerage's cornerstone belief. What she found was that the homespun local ads came nowhere close to producing the majority of an agent's business. After she was able to verify her findings, management was forced— and as you might imagine, this wasn't easy, considering the company's long-standing belief—to change its strategy.

It was only when the brokerage applied a working scorecard to its tactics that it was able to be influential in a way that was genuinely beneficial.

Make It Yours!

Managers may feel a certain futility from time to time about whether, and to what extent, they can "control" their people. We all would like more control over just about everything: the weather, airline travel, the rising price of gasoline, our putting stroke. The list is practically endless. At work, in our businesses, we'd feel a lot more secure if we had near total control.

But the evidence in today's ever-changing society, especially as we approach circumstances of nearly full employment, does not reflect that possibility. Controlling the behavior of our workers in a classic or traditional sense is little more than a false hope and will only buy us headaches, ulcers, daily frustrations, and dashed expectations. We really need to get comfortable with the fact that if we want to be highly compensated—whatever the currency—we're only going to be compensated in inverse proportion to how much we can control and in direct proportion to how much we can influence and, in the end, affect impact.

Only as we let go of the need to command and control do we make our lives easier and expand the empowerment of our people.

If we really have exercised positive influence, our influence will perpetuate and we will have a greater opportunity to manage that which we do not have a chance to observe.

The Concepts of Scorekeeping

17

MACRO TO MICRO

*If the whole is complete,
then the parts are working.*

Common Sense Coaching

When we open the sports pages and look at the headlines, what we always get in the big bold type at the top is who won and who lost. It's what's at the top of the page, the most important news, that matters above all else.

If we read farther into the news articles, invariably we'll soon wind up with the final score. That's important information too, but, within the context of the sports page, it's of secondary importance to who won and who lost.

Finally, if we want to find out the individual results of our favorite player, or perhaps our own son or daughter, we need to move even farther into the story, down to what they call the agate. That's the smallest size print and it holds the details of how individuals did in the contest. The natural order of things is from big to little, from macro to micro.

Getting to the Top

For centuries, a mountain peak that separates Nepal and Tibet sat at the top of the world, untouched and ignored.

It wasn't until 1852, when a British surveying team calculated that the mountain the natives call *Sagar-matha* was the highest point on earth, that anyone paid any attention to wanting to go there.

And it wasn't until 1953, when New Zealand mountain climber Edmund Hillary finally figured out a way to get all the way to the top of that 29,028 foot mountain, that "Mount Everest" (named after British surveying chief George Everest) became an active goal of the vertically inclined. In the years since, hundreds have scaled the world's tallest peak and hundreds others have died trying—all of them lured there by the mythical "guest register" they can sign their names to once they've made it to the top.

Every year, the waiting list grows of those waiting for permits to challenge Mount Everest. The demand easily exceeds the supply. And yet, no one is forced, or even ordered, to give it a try. The pursuit is universally voluntary.

The evolution of "climbing Mount Everest" is a good "macro to micro" model companies would be wise to follow when establishing scorekeeping systems. Note these steps: First, a goal was defined and established by "management" (when the British surveyors identified Mount Everest as the world's highest mountain). Second, someone in leadership demonstrated a willingness and enthusiasm to pursue, and eventually accomplish, the goal (Hillary's summit). And third, others, lured by the thrill of the challenge and the competition, followed in the leader's footsteps (those waiting in line to climb the mountain).

The scorekeeping system in place on Mount Everest is a simple one—that mythical guest register at the top is the only scorecard— but that simple system has proved more than enough for mankind to establish the goal of reaching the top of the mountain, and generate ample motivation toward the accomplishment of that goal.

Sam the Man

Sam G. is a warehouse manager in Los Angeles with 147 Teamsters under his command. One day he gets a directive from the people in corporate safety that says that, effective immediately, every warehouse employee has to wear a hardhat.

Now if you've ever used the phrase "have to" with a teamster, you know this isn't going to be easy. So Sam wonders, "How am I going to get this done?"

Like any good manager and leader of men, Sam mulls it over for a while until he finally hits on an idea. He goes out and buys a single hardhat, in his size, in shiny steel, and he has the people at the hardhat shop print a title in calligraphy on the front, just above the rim, that says: SAM THE MAN.

The next morning he wears his new hardhat to work. He doesn't say anything, there are no announcements, he just shows up and goes about his work as usual. No big deal.

You can imagine all the warehouse humor heaped on Sam. "Hey Chrome Dome!" "Why spend money to put a hat on your head when your head is harder than the hat?!" That kind of thing. But as the workday wears on and the teasing dies down, supervisors reporting to Sam come up to him and ask, "What's up? Why are you wearing that hardhat, Sam?" Their curiosity is now piqued.

"Well," he tells them, "I've examined IQ rates at warehouses and realized why nobody wears a hardhat." Sam is half-joking with them, of course, but he has their attention, and then he sets the hook further by adding, "Besides that, when I've got the hat on, everybody knows I'm in charge. There's a measure of authority that goes with wearing this hat."

The supervisors, already beginning to buy-in to this idea that hardhats make sense, then tentatively ask, "Are we going to get them?"

Sam, still setting the hook, responds cleverly, "If I can get them for you, will you wear them?"

After they all nod affirmatively, he says, "All right, this is the deal. We're all going to show up Monday with our hardhats on. Yours will be just like mine, with the title of your choice printed on the front. We'll all get teased, just like I did today. But after that dies down, we're going to give our list of reasons why we're wearing these things: they make the job safer and they add dignity to what we're doing."

The following Monday at 8 o'clock, Sam and all his supervisors show up wearing their hardhats. At 8:45, the rank and file threaten a work stoppage if they don't get hardhats too.

"If I can get them for you, will you wear them?" Sam asks, and every grizzled teamster in the crowd, 147 of them, answer, "Yes."

Sam Ganuscio got done in a heartbeat what might otherwise never have been accomplished, or might have resulted in disgruntlement and a schism between management and the ranks. Leading by example, he molded his unit into a team instead of into fragmented groups, each with its own agenda. And everybody wore their hardhats.

So exactly how does this tie into scorekeeping? It ties in because the same principle—leading by example—used by Sam for player buy-in also applies to implementing scorekeeping. We call it macro to micromanagement.

If I'm running a warehouse and I'm responsible for productivity per labor hour, and I decide that's an area where I need to keep score, then my first responsibility is to make sure I set up a scorecard for myself. I'll set up a system that shows how I'm doing, as the coach, in relationship to total team performance. With that in place, I'll also be in a position to compute the average team member performance. Our experience is that once I've gotten that far—once I've established an average—some of the players on the team (usually the best players) are going to come to me and say, "Hey, how am *I* doing?"

Then, like Sam with the hardhat, I'm in a position to set the hook and respond, "If I can get you the information, will you keep score on it?"

Scorekeeping is something that you have to make people *want* to do; something that you let your people do because you're doing it and it's appealing. **It's not something you make them do so you don't have to.**

> **Scorekeeping is something you make people want to do. It's not something you make them do so you don't have to.**

In its simplest form, then, macro to micro means we're going to look at scorecards for the entire team first before we get down into the micro-management of scorecards for any given player.

Let me offer a theoretical situation—one that parallels dozens of real-life cases from our GAME OF WORK files. Let's say I'm the manager of a retail outlet night crew that restocks the shelves every night. First I'll start out on the macro level and make a scorecard for the team leader, one that perhaps divides the total number of cases stocked by the labor hours used. That will effectively measure how the team leader is using all of the resources of the team.

The next thing I'll do is make certain I display that scorecard, taking care to keep it simple so it's obvious what the averages are. I'll put it in a prominent position so the team members can easily see it. When the team members then approach me and ask if they're better than the team average, that is when I act on the player's personal choice and give them the opportunity to create their own scorecards.

As we move into the micro part of the scorekeeping, the players will eventually list their scorecards as well—and I guarantee you that the evolution of personally chosen scorecards will beat forced competition every time.

Drilling Down

The overriding benefit of effective macro to micro management is that it facilitates a penetration, or a "drilling down," to take place. That in turn allows businesses, like dentists, to hit the nerve, find the pain, and fix the problem.

One of our GAME OF WORK clients, a distribution company, employed what on the surface appeared to be a fairly good indicator of productivity and profitability. The scorecard they devised measured the total cost of delivering an order versus the total profitability contained in that order. The right things were measured, and it was all positive relative to the goal.

But, still, it didn't work very well, this company discovered, because these overall scorecards weren't broken down at various levels so they could get a better picture of just what was going on in the operation. The company wasn't even sure if these scorecards accurately reflected real efficiency and productivity.

Only by constantly "drilling down" and getting to the core of the scorecard did this company's management make sure that certain variables hadn't skewed the scorekeeping. For example, because of an industry-wide price hike due to a shortage of product, the distribution side still "scored" well on a total dollar basis despite not moving as much product. Only by breaking down the scorecard so distribution could be judged on something more basic, such as dollars-per-order, could this quirk be dealt with and eliminated. Further drilling meant a clarification as to which shifts were the most efficient, and what days, allowing for scorecards that increased efficiency and productivity by responding to the variables involved in those areas.

Continuing this process of drilling down eventually produces a level where the scorecard clarifies the appropriate action for improvement. It is when we move in the right direction, from macro to micro, that we discover the secrets of good management as well as good scorekeeping.

Make It Yours!

The best conceived, most accurate, up-to-date, and foolproof scorekeeping system will fail without buy-in by the entire team, and that buy-in needs to be generated from the top. Good management dictates that scorecards be established like gravity, from top to bottom, not the other way around, and that everyone involved understands this.

Is your scorekeeping set up from the top down? Does management adhere to the scoreboard as well as the players? Does management lead by example? Do your scorecards keep "score" in varying degrees at varying levels? Examine them and make sure.

Make sure that each scorecard connects to the level above and the level below.

18

FREQUENT
ENOUGH TO FIX

*Frequent feedback builds player buy-in
and execution and breaks down problems
into manageable size.*

Common Sense Coaching

By the yard it's hard, by the inch it's a cinch."
We've all heard this saying since we were barely a yard tall,
that the growth process is cellular, that most progress occurs step-
by-step, not in leaps and bounds. Yet, because of past practices and
technological shortfall, we find ourselves bound in many instances
by scorecards that are limited to accounting practices created in the
latter half of the 19th century. Or, much like our prehistoric ances-
tors, we are limited or controlled by the phases of the moon.

The reality is, if I have a scorecard I am only reporting on once
a year—for example, after tax net earnings in a business—if I do
not succeed at refining and improving that scorecard, and making
it more frequent, then I have no opportunity to fix it and the problem is going to only get bigger.

A major credit card company that does not want us to leave
home without it has reported credit losses of almost $400 million a
year, a number deemed virtually too big to fix by anybody's standards because it's reported on an annual frequency. But what happens if we break that number down and recognize that it represents
about $1 million per day? That's still not an inconsequential num-
ber, but it's one that is a much more manageable figure. While the
problem is still formidable, it is now within the context of day-to-
day instead of once-a-year scorekeeping and is at least approach-
able.

Frequent attention can produce results previously believed
impossible.

Surpassing the Great Spitz

In Oklahoma City, I did some work with a company that does consulting work. This particular organization was going through a major transition period. After years in the retail business, it switched to consulting and was suddenly doing $400 million annually in revenue. You know the movie, *Honey I Blew Up the Kid*? That was the condition this company was in: all of a sudden they were huge, but they only had the motor skills of an infant.

After discussing their concerns over their growing pains, I said, "You need more frequent feedback and more frequent scorekeeping in your system."

They responded that their standard accounting processes, the ones they'd used for years, measured everything on a monthly basis. I said, "You don't have to be bound by the frequency of reporting that was imposed on you from past practice. If you want to be successful, you need to get your own measurement system; a measurement system that's meaningful for *you*, that gets *your* job done."

As the managers of this company stared at me, attempting to assimilate what I'd just said, trying to imagine something very difficult—doing business differently than *it had always been done before*—I knew I needed a good example to help make my point. So I told them one of my favorite stories about "frequent scorekeeping"—the one about Olympic swimming champion John Naber.

When John Naber came on the Olympic scene as a swimmer in the Montreal Games in 1976, it wasn't exactly great timing. In the Olympics held four years earlier in Munich, Mark Spitz had won an all-time Olympic high of seven gold medals while setting a world record in every race he swam. You can't get much more perfect than that.

The formidable problem for Naber, and for every other swimmer in Montreal, was how do you outswim Mark Spitz's shadow? How do you surpass *that*?

But John Naber set that as his goal just the same. And not only did he set the goal, he set up a meticulous plan for realizing that goal.

Naber was 16 when Spitz won all his medals and set all the records in Munich. As soon as those Olympics were over, the day they ended, the teenager and his coach calculated exactly how many days they had to work with, how many practice opportunities, how many warmup meets, before the next Olympics were scheduled to begin.

Next, they calculated how far Naber's times were from Spitz's times, as well as the other gold medalist swimmers in Munich.

From those calculations Naber was able to develop his own personal scorecard, one that allowed him to chart his progress against the progress he knew he'd need to become "The next Mark Spitz."

For four years of hard training he stuck to his scorecards. When he was ahead of pace, he would breathe a sigh of relief and celebrate; when he dropped behind pace he would consult with his coach and determine what needed to be changed, tweaked, or accelerated in his training to get back on track.

By the time Naber got to Montreal, he was at his peak. Not only were his goals as firmly in place as ever, but due to his personal scorekeeping system, he was confident that if he performed at his best he could set new world records.

Of the five events he entered, three were events Spitz had also entered in Munich, and in all three Naber exceeded what Spitz had recorded four years previous. (In one of those events, the 100-meter freestyle final, yet another swimmer, Bruce Furniss, also exceeded Spitz's world record and edged Naber for the gold medal by two-tenths of a second).

In all, John Naber collected four gold medals, one silver medal, and four world records at the Montreal Olympic Games. When the United States Olympic Hall of Fame was established a few years later, he was included among the charter group of inductees.

By devising a scorekeeping system that he believed in, that allowed him to "win" not just in the end, but at increments along the way, and that gave him frequent enough feedback that he could fix what needed to be fixed, John Naber was able to scorekeep his way to success.

As I said to the consulting firm, "The Olympic Games only measure every four years, but John Naber developed his own system of measuring. He needed feedback much more frequently than four years. He needed regular feedback so he could be successful when those four years were up."

Registry

As John Naber would no doubt be the first to attest, frequent feedback shrinks problems so they don't appear insurmountable. The more frequent the scorekeeping—and hence the feedback—the smaller the problems; the smaller the problems, the more doable the solution; the more doable the solution, the more motivated the player is to do those things necessary for success.

Many times there is nothing wrong with the scorekeeping, except its frequency. It's not the "how," it's the "how often."

Sometimes there is nothing wrong with the scorekeeping, except its frequency. It's not the "how," but the "how often."

At THE GAME OF WORK, we have found great value in taking the very same scorecards already in use, and by simply increasing the frequency of the feedback we discovered it's possible to generate significantly better results.

For example, in a major West Coast hospital, they were spending over a quarter of a million dollars every month on unscheduled overtime and what is called "registry." Now registry is a fancy industry-specific term for calling the temp help agency for nurses when the nurses who are scheduled can't or don't show up for one reason or another.

The problem is that the per-hour cost for registry nurses is substantially higher than the per-hour cost when regular nurses are used. Also, overtime costs are double the regular rate. For the hospital, this was a very expensive process. As is the case in most hospitals, registry was reported on a monthly basis—and it was a huge number. Huge enough for most people to look at and simply say, "Too big to fix." The size of the problem, encouraged by the infrequency of how often it was looked at, created a perception of "too large," "too difficult to solve," "practically impossible to change."

We implemented a scorekeeping process that was essentially unchanged from what the hospital had traditionally used. But now, instead of monthly reports, the scorecards kept track on not just a daily basis, but a shift-by-shift basis. Mostly, all we changed was the frequency.

It only made sense that overtime or registry needs wouldn't just occur on the last day of the month, or on the last shift of the day. By establishing 90 scorecards—one for each of three shifts for every day of the month—instead of three (one for each shift per month), we were able to chart the patterns of overtime and pinpoint the problem areas: those shifts that really blew the registry budget.

We now had the capability, the wherewithal, the commitment, and the perception, to determine where change was needed; to identify which shifts were causing the most problems. In addition to that, the director of patient services, who was responsible for nursing budget costs and productivity, was able to slice the information even further to reconfigure it into specific scores for each shift. As a result of all this, the problems on a shift basis became specific enough and small enough to attack.

The resulting proactivity enabled this hospital to double the number of shifts on which no overtime was required, and to save almost two-thirds of the previous overtime premium costs. Good news—unless you happened to be the temp agency.

Make It Yours!

As Thomas S. Monson, a leader in the Church of Jesus Christ of Latter-day Saints, was quoted in our GAME OF WORK book, "When performance is measured, performance improves. When performance is measured and reported back, the rate of improvement accelerates." I'd like to add the Coonradt corollary to that wisdom: "When you increase the frequency of the feedback, you will almost always get an improvement in the behavior that is measured."

Go find your important monthly scorecard and begin to look at it on a daily basis. You might say that you can't get that feedback or that you can't get it until the end of the month. But find a way to go and get it. I guarantee you'll find answers, maybe to a question you haven't even asked.

The Concepts of Scorekeeping

19

WHEN IT MATTERS

The player needs to know the score while the game is in progress.

Common Sense Coaching

Have you ever stood on the 17th tee when you and your partner are playing a best-ball match and you're two holes behind with just two holes to go?

There's only one thing you can do in that situation: Press the bet. Which is polite talk for "Double-or-nothing and see if we can get out of this deal with what we came with." Once you've made that decision, you stand up to the ball, hitch your pants á la Arnold Palmer, smack the ball as hard as you can á la John Daly, and then you and your partner have the opportunity for a bonding experience as you both drop to your knees and pray the ball doesn't go in the lake.

What you have just done is experience an important dynamic of correct scorekeeping—the heart-starting yet curiously exhilarating sense of purpose that comes with knowing the score before time runs out.

What makes the last two minutes of a close basketball game so exciting? What makes the final two minutes in football so much more exciting than the final two minutes in soccer, when the players are not allowed to see the time clock and are given no information as to when time will expire? It's that ability, that gift, that power, to be able to do something about the score while there's still time.

On Ice

Ice hockey and figure skating are both extremely competitive and skillful sports performed on ice rinks. But the way they keep score is as different as fire and ice. In hockey, you get one point every time the puck goes in the net. It's a running, completely current score updated instantly.

In figure skating, however, there is no instant scoring. Each competitor must go through his or her entire routine, and then wait for the judges to make their marks. Unlike hockey players, figure skaters do not have the opportunity to see if they're winning or losing while the competition is underway. Nor do they have the chance to change their behavior accordingly.

The vastly different atmospheres at hockey games and figure skating meets reflect this difference in scoring. A hockey game is boisterous, exciting, dynamic, loud; the ebbs and flows of the game constantly reflect the ebbs and flows of the score. But in figure skating meets, the mood, by contrast, is quiet, subdued, tense. There are few ebbs and flows and considerably less ongoing excitement.

I like to ask companies: "Is your scorekeeping more like figure skating or ice hockey?"

Would you rather have your players know what the score is while the game is going on so they can change their behavior and have a chance to win before time runs out, or would you rather keep them in the dark until the end of the sale period, the close of the fiscal year, or some other arbitrary finish line?

Watching TV

I remember a highly publicized boxing match that took place where Sugar Ray Leonard was fighting Tommy "The Hit Man" Hearns. Now in boxing, the scorekeeping is not current. It's like ice skating. No one knows the official score until the end of the bout. But in this particular fight, someone from Sugar Ray's corner was monitoring what was being reported by the television commentators, and the word from the TV was that even though Sugar Ray had staggered Hearns a couple of times, and nearly knocked him out in the 13th round, he was still behind on points.

Between the 13th and 14th rounds, Leonard's handlers relayed this information to him. They told him "what the score was," and, based on its ominous warning, recommended going for the knockout if Sugar Ray wanted to win. Sugar Ray needed to go for broke.

Which is exactly what he did. Abandoning any strategy of winning on points, Sugar Ray instead went all out for the knockout. As a result, down went Hearns with a little more than a minute remaining in the 14th round.

It turned out Leonard's TV "spies" were right. A check after the fight revealed that going into the 14th round their man was indeed behind on all three of the judges' cards, and could not have scored enough points in the final two rounds to win the fight. Knowing the score—or in this case, *guessing* the score—made all the difference.

I've often wondered, what if they were to change the scoring system in boxing so the contestants knew what the score was after every round? Would it change the behavior of the participants? Of course it would. Would it make it a better sport? I think so.

No Such Thing As "All of a Sudden"

One of my personal beliefs is that there ain't no such thing as "all of a sudden." A point I thought was driven home dramatically a few years ago when IBM, while experiencing growing pains, announced it was going to lay off 70,000 employees.

Many industry observers saw this massive cutback as occurring "overnight." But it only stood to reason that IBM had to lose focus along the way to get to the point that the jobs of 70,000 people became "suddenly" expendable. To get to that position, a lot of people—management and players—had to have lost sight of how they could win. They were like a boxer, blithely making his way through the rounds, with no clear idea if he had any realistic chance of actual winning.

My guess is that if we went back a number of years, we'd find a gradual decaying process. We'd find a steadily negative return for the company per employee expenditure. Otherwise, there's no way to explain how we could wake up one morning and magically have 70,000 people we don't need any more.

The tragedy is when no method of scorekeeping is in place to identify the stagnation and give us the chance to do something about it before "suddenly" comes along and wipes out half the workforce.

It's common to hear a company say that "all of a sudden" they had a longtime employee who quit. But if you were to find that employee and ask the reason for departure, he or she would typically say something like, "I just had enough." And the next response would be something like, "Well, for about the last ten years ..." And then it will all come out—the decay, the inattention to what was going on, the frustration that mounted, finally culminating with the termination of a relationship, whether by the employee's choice or the management's, because it no longer carries any value. Yet over and over again you'll hear companies insist that, "All of a sudden he just left."

All of a sudden means you haven't been watching the scoreboard.

Make It Yours!

Is your scorekeeping system dynamic and current? Does it build player enthusiasm, player motivation, and player performance? Does it ensure that everyone knows what the score is when there is still time to do something about it? In sports, that's what

> **The tragedy is when no method of scorekeeping is in place to identify the stagnation and give us a chance to do something about it before "suddenly" comes along and wipes out half the jobs.**

packs stadiums, that's what sends TV ratings soaring. In business, that's what will maintain employee morale and a buy-in that is current, vibrant, and responsive.

Resolve today to pick the most important scorecard in your organization that still resembles figure-skating and turn it into a daily, minute-to-minute dynamic, and watch your enthusiasm grow, not just proportionately, but disproportionately, to a higher level than you've ever seen before.

Create Your Own Scorecards

20

DATA TO PICTURES

"One picture is worth more than ten thousand words."
(ANCIENT CHINESE PROVERB)

Common Sense Coaching

If a picture is worth 10,000 words, then a pictoral scorecard must be worth a million bytes of data.

We think in pictures. We relate to pictures. We respond to pictures. If I say the word "football," a picture occurs in everyone's mind. For one person, it might be the view of a couch-potato husband on a Sunday afternoon, wearing out the batteries in the remote control. For another person, it might be holding the ball in victory after scoring a touchdown. For someone else, it might be the recollection of cuddling with a date under a big stadium blanket surrounded by 75,000 screaming fans. It will be different things for different people, but that one word will produce pictures in our minds, and those pictures will generate responses.

We value pictures. We trust pictures. We let pictures guide and direct us. It's been said that the eyes are the understanding sense. We leave the skepticism to our ears. We believe and buy in to what we can see.

When it comes to scorecards, seeing is also believing. The more we can really see, the better. Whenever we can take what begins as sterile data and translate that data into a graphic, living table, the better off we'll be at understanding what the score means to us.

Seeing is Entertaining

To appreciate the value of a "picture" scorecard, turn to any sports section in any newspaper in the country. Graphs and charts and other design devices are constantly being used, and with increasing frequency, to make a race or contest easier to understand.

During the summer and fall of 1998, when Roger Maris's home run record was hotly pursued by two big league baseball players, the race took on added interest by the publication of graphics that made the chase more understandable to a broader spectrum of the public. Much more than mere numbers were used to show just where each participant in the "race" stood.

Similarly, every summer when the Tour de France bicycle race is held, the race takes on added interest and relevance by charts, route maps and other devices that make it easier for the average person to relate.

The Information Age

Those of us older than 35 can lay fair claim to having lived through one of the most awe-inspiring ages of discovery in the history of mankind: The "Information Age."

The Information Age lifted off as the '60s were merging into the '70s and the computer industry introduced what we called Electronic Data Processing, or EDP. EDP used a lot of cards and created positions such as key punch operators, card punchers, and card readers. We used to take invoices and set them in front of someone like a typist and he or she would enter the information in. By punching holes in cards, the EDP machine would transform huge stacks of invoices into huge stacks of cards that would then be run through the computers to create huge stacks of paper. There were lots of printouts on 11" by 17" paper in the early days of EDP, creating the need for what were called data trolleys—those little wagons that would roll around the office, from the EDP department to the manager's office, and all points in between.

The EDP operators would typically leave their stacks of papers with a wave of the hand and a "The info's in there someplace, pal, good luck finding it." EDP was progress, but it was bulky progress.

Soon enough, EDP gave way to the era of Management Information Systems, or MIS, which took the information directly off the card decks and scanned it directly onto big discs, where it would stay until someone wanted to access the information. MIS eliminated the data trolleys, saved a few rain forests, and stored what was then an amazing amount of information. It usually stayed that way—stored. Like Johnny Carson used to say when he did his Carnack routine, "There's everything in the world you could possibly want to know if you only knew how to unlock it." Those who understood how to unlock the mysteries of MIS, and there weren't that many, became invaluable. "We can get that," or "If we need to find that out we can look that up," became the familiar phrases of the MIS era.

All of this, of course, was a prelude to the advanced computer age we find ourselves living in as we enter the 21st century, a time of microchips, the internet, e-mail, and computerized faxes that move at the speed of light. In much less than half a century, we have seen information retrieval go from the ice age to the jet age, metaphorically speaking. Our ability to produce, and assimilate, information has become as easy as "booting up" our personal computer.

I offer this short Information Age history lesson because it serves as background for discussing the importance of taking the abundance of information we have and doing something meaningful with it so that it gets noticed. Even though we may have more data than ever before, and indeed, more data than we might possibly ever need or use, it's going to be no good unless we can see it. We need to turn our data into pictures.

The real power in scorekeeping is when we take this abundance of information and turn it into what we call Action Stimulating Knowledge, or ASK.

ASK means that when a player is shown the scorecards that reflect current behavior, the player will then use that information to stimulate and movitate new behavior that will produce even better results.

We want to create scorecards that enable us to go from raw data, to information, to Action Stimulating Knowledge, to higher productivity. Just as it did no good back in the EDP or MIS days if the information was all there but beyond the normal person's reach, it does no good if we keep the scorekeeping information locked in our computers as uninterpreted data.

We talked earlier about the importance of scorekeeping preceding goalsetting. I used an example of expanded scorekeeping on my golf game that was considerably more meaningful, in terms of helping me improve, than merely looking at my average score for an 18-hole round of golf and deciding I wanted to lower my average. I talked about the significance of breaking down my game into a number of categories, i.e. how I did on the par 5's, the par 4's and the par 3's, respectively, and how I performed, in relationship to par, when it came to areas such as putting, driving, hitting fairways, and hitting greens in regulation.

What I didn't detail was the rest of the story—how I transferred all of my data into pictures. Dissecting my golf game into subsections wasn't enough. To complete my scorekeeping it remained for me to graphically reproduce my data onto scorecards that clearly showed me where I stood and just as clearly showed me where I most needed to improve. Only when I was armed with picture scorecards was I in a position to use my data effectively.

Just as Expected

An electric sign company told us that for years they had experienced problems with their accounts receivable. Payments from clients were habitually late, but no one knew exactly how late, and to add to the problem, over the years an attitude of "it's just something we have to live with" had been established within the company. Late payments were just part of being in business. That was the attitude.

The billing process, which came from accounting, kept track of the usual overdue categories, which ranged from the typical cycles of 0-30 days, 31-60 days, 61-90 days, 90-120 days, and over 120 days. These divisions of what is commonly called "aging" were the same used by most businesses. "Aging" is kind of the Latin language of business in that it's a dead language. It does not produce much activity and it is typically reported in numerics.

After studying THE GAME OF WORK curriculum and gaining an understanding of the need for better feedback, this company decided to take a more proactive stance. The people in accounting got together with the people in the computer room and they succeeded in collecting data on all of the money that had ever been deposited with the company, and when. As you can see on the illustrations, they began by taking the current month and plotting backward, and that allowed them to finally come up with a historical document that showed the company's monthly cash flow.

After plotting the first month, they saw a rather soft curve occur in the pattern of dollars received. Instead of a straight line, signifying steady payments, they noticed there was an infusion of cash toward the sixth banking day of the month, then a slump. They plotted another month and noticed the same. And then another. And another. Overall, the graphics showed that there was a consistent pattern for receipt of funds.

These results confirmed suspicions that many in management had held for years but had never acted upon because there was no hard information to verify anything. But now, armed with the data displayed by the graphs, they could capably predict the pattern of cash flow into the business. This gave their collection people a daily awareness of what to expect, allowing them to create programs and appeals for cash far earlier in the sequence than previously had been anticipated. As a result, the company quickly reduced its uncollected accounts payable by almost four full days of sales revenue, due to a more efficient and increased collection system.

Daily Deposits

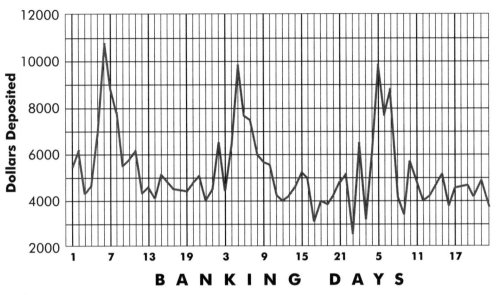

It was all because they could finally see what was going on around them. Turning the data into pictures made all the difference.

Make it Yours!

To turn your data into pictures, take advantage of the age of wonders in which we live. With personal computers at our fingertips, with the internet, instantaneous e-mail, voice mail, call-waiting, cell phones, facsimile machines, printers and copy machines, we have fewer excuses than anyone in the history of business to not be "on top of things." The data is at our fingertips. The challenge to us is to make it, as the computer companies would put it, user-friendly. Turn that data into scorecards that are, above all, extremely user-friendly.

The big word now is knowledge. Just jump on the net and look at "knowledge management" or "knowledge business". Those are the hot new buzz phrases. Focus on your Action Stimulating Knowledge. There is no excuse today for us to produce confusing reams of numbers which force the viewer of those numbers to hunt and peck for the gems of wisdom that are hiding within. Even if you're not electronically enhanced or proficient, the few extra moments required to turn data into an Action Stimulating Knowledge-based scorecard is well worth the investment.

Create Your Own Scorecards

21

LINE THEM UP

It's not only how your perform, but how you compare.

Common Sense Coaching

*N*ow *that we've established the fundamental points of score-keeping and the tremendous value of pictures, let's move into the construction phase of the process.*

First, let's establish this rule: no matter what the activity, the basics of scorecard building remain the same. The fundamentals that apply and work in your business and personal circumstances are the same as those that apply and work for a Super Bowl-winning football team, baseball's batting champion, or an Olympic gold medalist.

Sports teams have a long and productive history of using properly designed scorecards to apply to individual situations instead of generalities. In the National Football League, for example, the average gain per play is right around five yards. If you take yards per passing play and yards per running play the overall average is about five yards.

But when you break that down, you find that the average per passing play is about seven yards and the average per running play is about three. And those are the numbers that are applied to the individual players. The pass receivers are scored according to the seven-yard average while the running backs are scored according to the three-yard average. Everything is kept relevant.

If you were to take all the pass receivers and the running backs and tell them that if their personal average per play was above five yards then they are better than average, what would you get? You'd get a lot of happy receivers and a lot of running backs trying to get their hands on your throat, right? The receivers would think, "This is a sweet deal. We can't lose," and the running backs would think, "There's no way to win here." Either way, the reaction stemming from such thoughts would probably not be an asset to the team.

The receivers, thinking they are well above average, would be motivated to do less, and the running backs, thinking there's no way they can average five yards a play, would quit trying.

But no NFL team does that. They're going to break down the statistics and make them relevant. They get very exact about it, as a matter of fact. Based on individual scorecards that are relevant, a pro football team is going to have a different yardage quota for each one of its yardage-gainers. You know they're going to do that. Why? Because it's fair, and because it demands the right kind of production per player and position. There's no way a tailback is going to have the same yardage expectation as a fullback or, for that matter, as a wide receiver. If you're Emmitt Smith, your scorecard is going to give you different averages, and expectations, than if you're Moose Johnson, or Michael Irvin. It's all relative and relevant.

It's as Simple as AMR

As we go through the simple, straightforward steps to constructing a basic scorekeeping line graph, it will be beneficial to consult the accompanying illustrations, enabling you to visually grasp the elemental concepts. Please be assured, you don't need a degree in math to construct a perfectly sound line graph scorecard. As you'll soon discover, there is nothing difficult about this procedure.

The first step in building a scorecard is to plot what we call the Actual line. By definition, the Actual line means actual performance or production. It might be today's production per labor hour, it might be performance in a particular event, or it might be a sales presentation. Actual refers to what actually happened today in an actual event.

Let's say I'm a college student and I want to construct a graphic scorecard that shows my math test scores. The first thing I'll want to do is set up a basic line graph, including a time line across the bottom and a volume line rising vertically on the left side of the graph.

With these two lines in place I can then create my Actual line by plotting my test scores according to time (the date the test was taken) and volume (my score).

If I score an 82 on, let's say, Sept. 1, an 83 on Sept. 5, a 91 on Sept. 10, a 76 on Sept. 15, and so on, I'll make those marks on the graph. By connecting these dots I'll create my Actual line. It will rise and fall as it makes its way from left to right across the page. Because of the wide range in my test scores, this horizontal line will have a good deal of variation to it.

By plotting my Actual line, I can now see the ups and downs of my test scores. But I am by no means finished. The Actual line is just the first step in constructing my scorecard.

Math Test Actual Scores

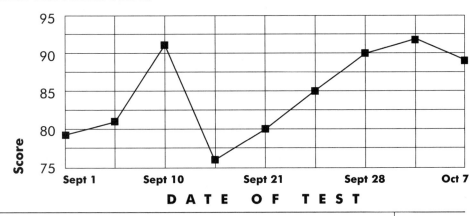

Next, I need to add a second line called the Mean line.

The Mean line lets me know my accumulative average—an important piece of information that lets me see if my average test score is getting higher or lower.

The Mean line is computed simply by adding the individual numbers on the Actual line and dividing that total by the number of individual marks. In my college test scores example, if I add up my first four test scores, the total of 82, 83, 91 and 76 is 332. By dividing 332 by the number of marks (the number of tests taken,

Math Test Average Score

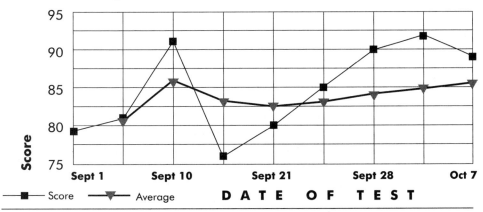

which in this case is four), I will get my average test score. Since 332 divided by four equals 83, my cumulative average is 83. I'll plot that on my Mean line corresponding to my fourth test.

I can similarly plot the other marks on the Mean line by adding the number of tests to that point on the graph and dividing by the number of tests. Thus, I can compute that my average after three tests is 256 divided by three, or 85.5; and after two tests it's 165 divided by two, or 82.5.

While my Actual line jumps from 82 to 83 to 91 to 76, my Mean line, which reflects my changing average test score, is going to move along at a steadier pace, going from 82.5 to 85.5 to 83.

This is all pretty simple math but very enlightening and beneficial because now we've got some emotion in our graph. By adding the Mean line, we begin to get a trend and a chronological perspective. The graph now tells me something I didn't already know. It tells me if I'm improving or not. It lets me know if I'm getting better over time, or worse. The Mean line serves as the interpreter for the Actual line.

It is the Mean line that allows me to take advantage of the concept of above- or below-average.

We all inherently know we want to be above-average.

The Mean line lets me know if I'm above or below average.

The simple addition of a Mean line establishes the basis for appropriate coaching.

The beauty of line graph scorecards is that they are applicable to anything we can put a number on, and they are simple to do.

Once we have our Actual and Mean lines in place, we're still not quite finished, however.

We need to add one more line to make sure our information—and therefore our feedback—is current. In addition to how we're doing overall, we need, most importantly, to know "How am I doing lately?"

We can find out by adding the Rolling line.

The Rolling line is computed by taking the data from our last five performances, dividing by five, and plotting those numbers on their own separate line.

The Rolling line is typically going to fluctuate less than the Actual line, but more than the Mean line.

The Rolling line becomes more and more important over time simply because the Mean line is going to flatten out the longer it gets, becoming harder and harder to disturb no matter how extreme an individual or daily result. Thus it becomes increasingly difficult

In addition to how we're doing overall, we need, most importantly, to know: How am I doing lately?

Math Test Last Five Rolling Average

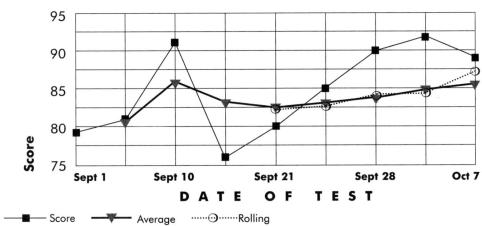

Legend: —■— Score   —▼— Average   ·····☉·····Rolling

to identify "how we're doing lately" with the Mean line. The Rolling line is what brings immediacy into the equation. In my college test scores example, I can use my Rolling average to gauge my current progress, my productivity *this week*. If I can continually maintain my Rolling average higher than my Mean average, I'll instantly know I am moving in the right direction.

The benefit of what we call AMR (Actual, Mean, Rolling) is that it allows clarity and recognition to grow out of the data. It paints a very clear picture. As more and more AMR data is calculated and filed, performance is much more sharply defined, as are the relative needs for coaching.

Apples to Apples

Once you have a grasp on the fundamentals and values of AMR, it's a quick leap to realize they are practically universally applicable. Once we devise a way to assign a numerical value to whatever it is we're doing, we're keeping score.

There is an important caution to be added, however, and it is this: be certain that each graph, or scorecard, computes similar, compatable data. I wouldn't want to use the math graph and mix in my test score averages for chemistry and literature, in other words. That wouldn't be useful. Instead, I'd want to have a separate graph for each. By combining dissimilar data we'll only succeed in distorting the results and limiting their usefulness. In order to be reliable, our scorecards first need to be equitable.

Let me use the restaurant business as an example.

Average Dollars Per Customer Per Day

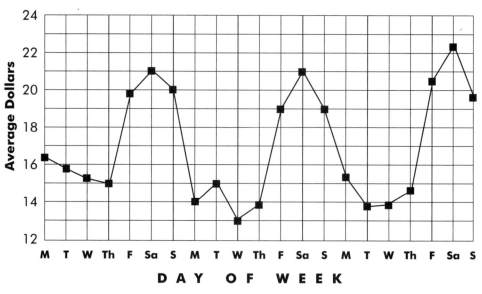

In the restaurant business, one of the most meaningful things to track is the average dollar spent by each customer. That's an important, and commonly used, indicator of how the business is doing. If you sell more appetizers, more desserts, a second or third beverage, and so forth, you're going to drive your transaction size up in spite of the limits placed by your fixed assets, which are the number of seats and square footage available. You can only fit so many people in the building, in other words, so the best way to build your business is to increase how much each person spends once they get in there.

If I'm running a restaurant and I want to set up a line graph scorekeeping system to help me see how I'm doing in dollars-per-customer I would first set up a graph with a time line listing each day on the bottom, or horizontal axis, and a volume line, listing average-dollars-per-customer, on the lefthand, or vertical, axis.

I would begin my plotting by taking the number of average dollars spent per customer per day and creating an Actual line that would stretch from left to right across the graph.

Next, I would add a Mean line by computing the cumulative average of dollars-per-customer and plotting those numbers on a daily basis as well.

The third step, of course, would be adding the Rolling line,

Average Dollars Per Customer Per Day

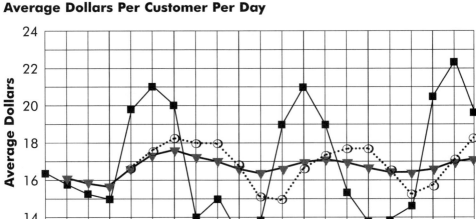

reflecting averages for the last five days.

This scorecard would give me a general overview of how the business is doing. But I wouldn't want to stop there. Since the restaurant business is a cyclical business by nature, my graph would undoubtedly reflect huge gyrations in average dollars per customer depending on the day of the week.

That wouldn't show that the people working in my restaurant are doing an erratic job. What it would show is that different days reflect different customer behavior. People just don't spend as much at a restaurant on a Tuesday or a Wednesday as they do on a Friday and Saturday. That's just the way the business works.

So I'd want to have one scorecard for Mondays, another for Tuesdays, and so on. That way, my scorecards would be relevant and appropriate.

Remember, the scorecard's primary objective is to get a coach and a player to agree not only on when, but on what kind of feedback is apropriate. If I created my restaurant scorecards and didn't make them credible, either everyone would grumble, or, more probably, I'd get the people responsible for Mondays grumbling and the

The scorecard's primary objective is to get a coach and player to agree not only on when, but on what kind of feedback is appropriate.

Dollars Per Customer Monday

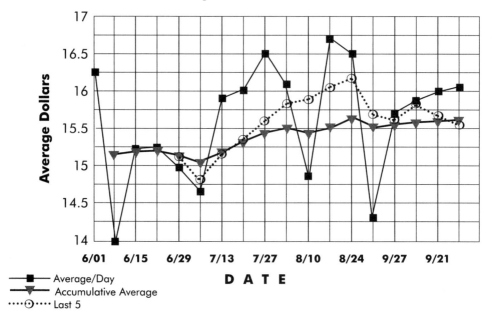

Average Dollars

- ■ Average/Day
- ▼ Accumulative Average
- ⊙ Last 5

D A T E

Dates: 6/01 6/15 6/29 7/13 7/27 8/10 8/24 9/27 9/21

people responsible for Saturday night thinking they don't have to work very hard because they're way above average.

Only by taking care to create separate scorecards for each day can I create an opportunity for everyone involved in my restaurant to win every day.

My scorecards need to be relevant. They need to inspire meaningful, constructive feedback between coach and player. They need to create an atmosphere of winning, making it possible not only for everyone to be able to win, but to see winning as a viable *reachable* possibility.

In the same way as our previous NFL example, if you're the manager of our restaurant on Monday night, you're going to have different averages, and expectations, than if you're our manager on Saturday night. A Monday average of $14-per-guest might be cause for celebration, while a Saturday average of $24-per-guest might be cause for rethinking and extra coaching.

It all goes back to the scorecard. If your scorecards are properly constructed, first with accurate Actual, Mean, and Rolling lines, and second with relevant, "apples-to-apples" data, they will give you the information you need to be able to accurately assess where you stand, and what you need to do to keep increasing your productivity.

Make it Yours!

Take the time to familiarize yourself with the simplicity of constructing Actual, Mean, and Rolling lines on a simple line graph. The few extra minutes it takes to add these statements of relevance will substantially enhance the communication value of the scorecard. Don't allow your scorecards to become "plot and shrug." (that means you draw a line on it, you look at it, you have no idea what that means, and you shrug your shoulders).

There is virtually no limit to what can be measured, in great detail, with these three lines. Apply them to the important areas in your business, and in your life, and watch as they create a picture for you that is clear and helpful. Basic, fundamental scorekeeping will bring life, and greater productivity, to whatever area in which you are seeking success.

22

THE DIFFERENCE BETWEEN WOW! & HOW?

There is a dearth of quality coaching in American business.

Common Sense Coaching

Most of us went through all of our college and most of our professional careers with little training in the area of coaching. Many of us have had courses on managing, direction, controlling, statistical processing, planning, and time management. But training designed to get managers to develop coaching skills as they relate to meaningful interraction with those they direct has been virtually nonexistent.

As a result, most of us don't know how to coach and more importantly, we don't know when.

Scorekeeping is the bridge that can help us begin to cross that training gap.

Scorekeeping tells us how to coach and when to coach.

With the right scorekeeping system in place, both player and coach can know what is expected—allowing for that clear and necessary distinction between what deserves to be celebrated and what needs to be corrected.

This need for an efficient relationship between coach and player is paramount. It cannot be overemphasized. The ability to deliver consistent and appropriate feedback is the most important human relation skill known to man. Conversely, the delivery of inappropriate feedback is the greatest morale slayer in our society.

Performance Standard

The scorecard decides if what we call the Performance Standard is being satisfied.

By definition, and you can better visualize this by looking at the accompanying illustration, Peformance Standard refers to satisfactory performance as predetermined by the company's values.

If a player's performance is below the Performance Standard it falls beneath what we refer to as the "line of demarcation" and the

Field of Play

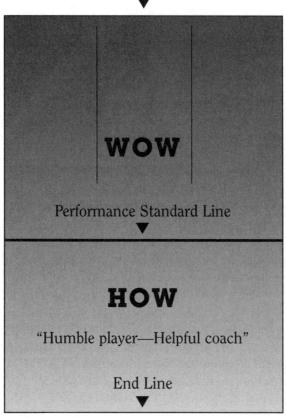

PAYDIRT

Goal Line
▼

Terminal
Out of
Bounds

Operational
Out of
Bounds

WOW

Performance Standard Line
▼

HOW

"Humble player—Helpful coach"

End Line
▼

PERFORMANCE OUT OF BOUNDS

coach knows there's a problem, and knows that it needs to be addressed.

If a player's performance hits above the line of demarcation, the coach knows things are headed in the right direction, and it's time to celebrate.

Thus coaching becomes an option of two three-letter words:

Wow! and *How?*

When players are in the *Wow!* zone, it means they are doing fine. Their performance is acceptable, definitely on the positive side of the line of demarcation.

In response, the coach will say, *"Wow!* Way to go! Great job! Congratulations!"

When players are in the *How?* zone, however, they are not meeting the performance standard. Their productivity is unacceptable, definitely on the negative side of the line of demarkation.

In response, the coach will ask, *"How* can I help?"

In a properly functioning scorekeeping situation, the *Wow!* and *How?* zones are clearly defined and understood.

When a player scores in the *Wow!* zone the coach is honor-bound to be excited and celebratory. That's the coach's job: to applaud, to give compliments, to cheerlead, to encourage more of the same. Even if the coach is not present when the score comes in, the player can rightly rely upon a predictably positive response as soon as the coach does become aware of the performance. In that instance, it's possible for the player to experience his or her own euphoria just knowing that the coach's response, when it comes, will reliably be positive.

On the other hand, if performance falls below the performance standard, the coach's response is also predictable. The appropriate feedback begins with *"How."* That's not a lead-in for, "How on earth could you have messed up this badly?" but, rather, *"How* can I help?" "What can I do?"

In partnership with the player, it is the coach's responsibility to bring to bear all of his or her expertise, creativity, experience, and knowledge to provide a plan of action and strategy that will produce the highest probability of the player elevating his game to the *Wow!* zone.

The role scorekeeping plays in the player-coach relationship is vital. By establishing predetermined performance levels it provides the coach with what he or she needs to endorse the behavior both player and coach want to see repeated. Scorekeeping that has a

> Coaching becomes an option of two three-letter words: Wow! and How?

commonly agreed upon line of demarcation between celebratory or "*Wow!*" feedback and instructional or "*How?*" feedback has the power to greatly improve communication, reduce uncertainty and resentment, and add to celebration opportunities within an organization.

It provides all the necessary boundaries—boundaries that ensure objectivity, fairness and clear goals. Scorecards don't just show performance standards, they keep them anchored. They don't allow them to drift. They make sure the subjectivity or whim of neither player nor coach allows the standards to move with no basis in fact. Gone are the days of confusion, of shifting expectations, of changing goals, of playing favorites and turning a blind eye. These are behaviors that can cripple and eventually undermine and destroy the best of businesses.

The *Wow!* and *How?* zones give coach and player a solid and common ground to work from. They define a coach's responsibilities, and give him or her the opportunity to facilitate productivity instead of just getting in the way.

I know that none of us has a burning desire to be overcoached. The last thing we want is someone standing over our shoulder making sure we dot all the i's and cross all the t's.

But a far greater sin, and the greatest disservice to the players in American business, is to undercoach—to leave people struggling with their assignments, in the dark about how they're doing and even about what they're supposed to be doing.

Remember, all of us, whether we're the janitor or the CEO, come to work every day wanting to know how to win. By knowing precisely where the *Wow!* zone ends and the *How?* zone begins, the answer to that question becomes perfectly clear.

One effective way I've found to visualize the *Wow!* and *How?* zones is to think of a football player carrying the ball. When he takes the ball from the quarterback and turns upfield, the objective is to make as many yards as possible.

If the run is a short one, producing a small gain or no gain at all, the player will find himself in the *How?* zone, and the coach is going to turn his attention to help that player gain more ground in the future.

If, on the other hand, the run is of some length, let's say at least five yards or so, the player will have then made it into the *Wow!* zone and he will receive appropriate encouragement and celebratory feedback from the coach.

Keeping this visualization in mind, now imagine the ball carrier making it all the way to the end of the field. He scores a touchdown! The desired end result has been achieved. It's time to celebrate!

Coaches in today's business world would do well to focus on the *Wow!* and *How?* zones. The days of the manager-as-cop, of lying in wait to "catch them doing it wrong," are over. Browbeating is a thing of the past. Verbal tirades are thankfully out of style.

For a number of reasons, that type of management style is quickly becoming "The Dark Ages." First, the number of enlightened managers that have proactively chosen not to allow that beratement mentality are moving into a majority of American businesses. Secondly, when unemployment levels are low, it creates a situation that offers sufficient alternative employment opportunities so that players don't have to put up with that beratement nonsense any more. Thirdly, corporate owners are wising up to the paradox between paying people premium wages and then expecting them to put up with substandard leadership.

End Lines and Goal Lines

I was a punter for my college football team. Whenever the team was in trouble I was called into the game. You don't have to know much about the game of football to know that a team doesn't punt until it is basically out of more agreeable options than giving away the ball.

A lot of times when I was called on to punt our team would be backed up close to the end zone. Now that end zone had different meaning for the two teams playing the football game. To the opposition, it represented scoring, touchdown, six points, meeting their goal. To the punting team, it represented failure, disappointment, uh-oh.

My job as punter was to get the other team as far away from success, and my team as far away from disaster, as possible. I needed to clear the other team away from what for them was the goal line, and what for us was the end line.

Because of their application to many goals and games we can all relate to, I like to use these two terms—End Line and Goal Line—to identify the extremes of the *Wow!* and *How?* zones as we complete the construction of our scorecards. (Again, you will be able to better visualize this concept by looking at the accompanying illustration in this chapter).

Note that the Goal Line represents the far end of the Wow!, or celebratory, zone. Crossing over the Goal Line means achieving the goal, and creating a clear cause for celebration.

The End Line represents just the opposite. It marks the beginning of the field of play. Beyond the End Line represents unacceptable behavior. When you go across it, you're off the field. That doesn't mean you're off the team, but it does mean you might be in for a change of assignment, or extra time with your coach.

The End Line represents the bare minimum. If I cross over the End Line it means my responsibility is going to change; and the closer I get to that border, the more "*How?*" questions will be communicated to me by my coach.

As long as both player and coach are aware where the player stands, the level of demand for appropriate coaching is going to be obvious. The danger of overcoaching diminishes and the value of necessary coaching feedback increases. I get coaching and feedback when I need it, not when the coach feels like it, or because of some corporate need for intervention that might be well intended but at the same time misguided.

As our illustration shows, whenever a player is in the well-defined area between the End Line and the Performance Standard, *How?* coaching will not be an option, it will be expected. And once a player crosses past the line delineating between the *Wow!* and *How?* zones, that's when the job descriptions change. Now a coach's assignment is to celebrate with the player, and the player's assignment—or privilege, if you will—is to celebrate his or her performance.

Paydirt

The Goal Line marks the beginning of that area of the scorecard we call paydirt.

In football, the area beyond the Goal Line is called the End Zone. The end zone is the place you want to go, it's just not that easy to get there.

Crossing the Goal Line and entering into the end zone is a culmination, a touchdown, a victory! It represents leaving the *Wow!* zone, where I'm virtually assured of keeping my job and getting positive feedback from my coach, and penetrating a higher level of celebration, where the victory is more final and secure. Distinctions of just exactly what constitutes crossing the Goal Line will vary from company to company and business to business, just as they vary from sport to sport and game to game. The important thing is that the Goal Line is clearly identified on our scorecard, so there is no question when it has been crossed. The goal line, once established, does not move.

By definition, making it across the Goal Line is going to be a big deal, and we have found it is advantageous for a company to reflect just how big a deal with a compensation change at that point. Certainly no one is likely to argue that superlative performance deserves superlative recognition, just as no one is likely to argue that the best kind of recognition is in some form of added compensation.

This added compensation can be direct or indirect. It can be in the form of a monetary bonus, or it can be in the form of non-paycheck related issues, i.e. comp time off, special privileges, the company's box seats for the symphony or a resident NBA team home game, or some other added benefit. It might translate into preferred parking in the company parking lot, or lunch at the best restaurant in town, or the use of the company jet. Its role is to represent company appreciation of performance well beyond what is expected.

Two guidelines for Goal Line compensation should be kept in mind.

First, the compensation needs to be fiscally responsible. It must fit into the cost structure in the company, and as an underlying guideline, it ideally should be a reflection that performance at this level is substantially more profitable to the organization because it goes far beyond fixed costs that have already been amortized.

Compensation needs to be fiscally responsible to the company and emotionally stimulating to the player.

Second, it needs to be emotionally stimulating to the player. One of the best ways to build emotional involvement is by allowing the player to preselect a tangible and specific payoff or payout should he or she cross the Goal Line. It could be a $5,000 bonus for one person, a family week at Disneyland for another, and for another it could mean a certificate of deposit earmarked for a child's college education. To yet another player it might mean a premiere shotgun, to another a mountain bike or some other piece of sporting equipment that doesn't usually fit into the family budget.

It has been our experience, incidentally, that bonuses "in kind" have proven to be much more meaningful, and motivational, than bonuses in hard, cold cash. We have found, time and again, that the number one response to cash bonuses is—you guessed it—to pay bills. Something we'd do anyway, if at a slower rate. The subconscious message is this: If you're extra successful, you're going to pay bills. If you're not ultra successful, you're going to pay bills. The message to your mind and your heart is—it makes no difference.

But if the bonus has some real allure ...

Cowboy Boots

I really like cowboy boots. I like the way they feel. I like the way they fit. I like walking in them.

My favorite brand of boot is called Luchesse. If you've ever seen a pair of Luchesse boots you wouldn't wonder why. They are top of the line, soft, pliable, luxurious, comfortable, virtually indestructible. The very best. My favorite is a full quill ostrich boot that Luchesse makes in a color they call black cherry, which is an unbelievably deep burgundy color. Black cherry Luchesse's sell for $899 a pair. I have a pair I bought over five years ago that I've worn probably three hundred times and they still look good.

There's no question that nine hundred dollars for a pair of cowboy boots is a bit of a stretch—a hard purchase to justify without zooming well past "necessity" and into outright luxury.

But those boots get my attention. They really get me going. So I've decided that when my royalty checks exceed a certain total, I'm going to buy those black cherry Luchesse ostrich quill boots. No matter what. That will be my reward.

Those cowboy boots give me something I can focus on, a visualization that works. I can get the stimulus I need from the boots to work harder toward my goal.

That's an effective compensation bonus for me. It's a lot more effective than if I was looking at a check, so I could have the opportunity to pay more bills.

In your life, what are your cowboy boots? More important, what are your players' cowboy boots?

The Bottom Line

The value of a properly constructed, current, relevant scorekeeping system cannot be overstated. With the use of pictures instead of raw data; line graphs that utilize the magic of Actual, Mean, and Rolling measurements in the place of the traditionally vague, complicated and impersonal corporate reports; and a well-defined playing field that clearly marks Performance Standard, End Lines, and Goal Lines (and the compensation change that goes along with them), virtually any endeavor can be changed from something undefined, uninspiring and unfulfilling into something that is vital, vibrant and, best of all, productive. It's the very same endeavor! The job description hasn't changed at all, just the perception and enthusiasm because scorekeeping has succeeded in transforming work into a game!

Productivity % to Target

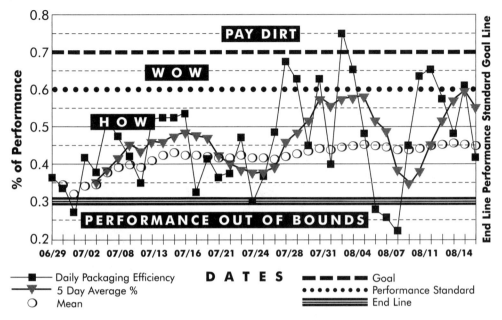

Make It Yours!

Is your business equipped with well established boundary lines? Do coaches and players alike know where those lines are? Is it common knowledge exactly what constitutes a Performance Standard, the *Wow!* zone and the *How?* zone? Is everyone aware when they've stepped off the End Line into the far end of the field, in jeopardy of dismissal or reassignment? Is everyone equally aware when they've crossed over the Goal Line, and gone beyond *Wow!* feedback to extra compensation (bonus) feedback?

By setting up an efficient, easy-to-maintain scorekeeping system, your business can be as easily staked out, and identifiable, as a football field in the NFL just prior to kickoff. No one will be unclear as to what is good field position, and what isn't. Establish these clear markings in your business, and see the dramatic changes that will occur as a result.

Create Your Own Scorecards

23

MAKE THEM BOUNCE

When it comes to scorekeeping, bigger is better.

Common Sense Coaching

*O*nce we've succeeded in including the proper ingredients in our scorecards, with the requisite Actual, Mean, and Rolling lines and with distinct delineations for Performance Standard, Wow! zones, How? zones, End Lines, and Goal Lines, we need to allow for plenty of room within the scorecard, ensuring that its information is easily seen.

To make this point, take a look at the scoreboard the next time you go to a sports stadium or arena. Unless you happen to go to Chicago and visit Wrigley Field, where the scoreboard used by the Chicago Cubs doggedly sticks to tradition, remaining virtually unchanged since the days when baseball teams regularly played day games and scores from other cities were relayed by telegraph, you're going to see scoreboards that tell you everything you want to know, and probably a lot more.

The rule of sports scoreboards is definitely Bigger is Better. Over the years, scoreboards have evolved to the point that they have become, in and of themselves, part of the entertainment. We now have big screen scoreboards in basketball and hockey arenas that televise the game even as it is in progress. As soon as a play is finished, we get to see it again on the scoreboard in instant replay. During timeouts, the scoreboard flashes pertinent statistical information. Throughout the game, we know who is scoring and doing what.

There is no reason our scoreboards in the workplace can't be similarly entertaining and enlightening. I'm not saying we should erect a JumboTron in the office lobby. By adhering to the concept that bigger is better—and clearer—what I am saying is we can get the very most out of our scorekeeping by making sure the scoreboards we use get our message across as loud and clear as possible.

We need to make our scoreboards, and our scorecards, bounce.

By "bounce," I mean make sure the scoreboard and scorecard clearly communicate the ups and the downs.

To visualize the following examples, please look at the accompanying illustrations in this chapter.

Let's say I'm the manager in a company's computer department and I've decided I want to create a scorecard that measures time. I create a line graph scorecard that measures the percentage of the time our computers are up and running. (Remember, in order to reinforce the behavior we want repeated, we need to measure the positive instead of the negative; hence, our scorecard is going to concentrate on the time our computers are fully functioning, not when they're shut down).

On the volume axis on the lefthand side of my scorecard I list percentages of up-time in one-degree increments, starting with a 0 at the base and 100 percent at the top of the graph. On the time axis that runs horizontally I've listed our days of operation.

Percentage of time on-line

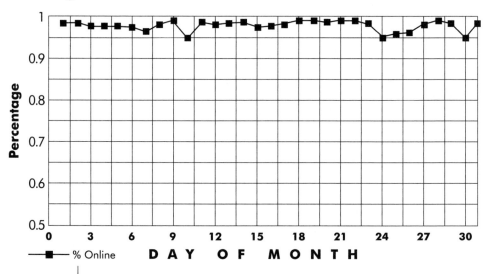

Because our computers typically run very efficiently, in the 95 to 99 percent range, when I plot my Actual, Mean, and Rolling lines, I find that I'm using only a small portion of the graph, located at the very upper end.

Now a one percent change in computer-use efficiency is a big deal in my business. If I can increase my average efficiency from, say, 96 to 97 percent, that translates into a significant increase in productivity and overall profit. So one percent is meaningful. One percent matters.

But my scorecard doesn't communicate that. My scorecard communicates that one percent represents a change that appears to be so small it is quite insignificant.

The remedy is simple. Instead of charting the percentages from 0 to 100, I need to reconstruct the scorecard so it reflects what's important. I need to have the leftside volume axis go from 90 to 100 percent, or even 93 to 98 percent. Whatever is necessary to maximize the amount of visualization and bounce in the lines.

Percentage of time on-line

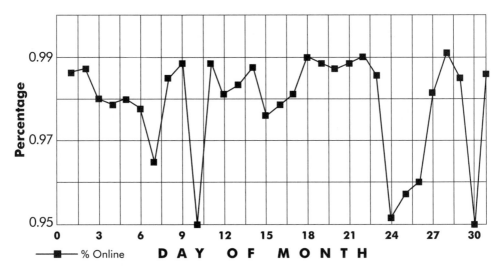

It's the bounce that adds interest and prompts celebration.

Let's use another example. Let's say I'm creating scorecards for a warehouse distribution center and I'm measuring the percentage of time I'm in stock with the right product and I have a goal to have that number be no less than 95 percent. If I move a tenth of a percentage point, that represents a significant level of accomplishment.

I need to take care that my scorecard does not reflect a tenth of a percentage point as some miniscule movement in the line. I need to construct "big screen" scorecards magnified enough so that tenths of percentages get their proper illumination.

Successful management is really nothing more than the sum total of making a big deal out of the little stuff we want more of.

Our scorecards should reflect this important principle. Little things add up. Consistency is what counts. Scorecards that reflect consistency and regular improvement promote more of the same.

The secret to getting the deal done is using the motivation of the big goal to overcome the small obstacle.

Take something as universal as weight loss. Most of us know we should eat better, healthier, and take off a few pounds. But if I really want to lose weight I need to first think of all the reasons I want to weigh 189 pounds again, which is what I weighed when I graduated from high school. "I will have more energy," "I'll live longer," "I can again fit into those 34-inch waist jeans" ... if that's what motivates me, and if I can keep that motivation in mind, THEN I can pass on the lemon meringue pie after dinner, or at least decline the urge to super size my order at McDonald's.

> **S**uccessful **management** is nothing more than the sum total of making a big deal out of the little stuff we want more of.

Percentage of time on-line

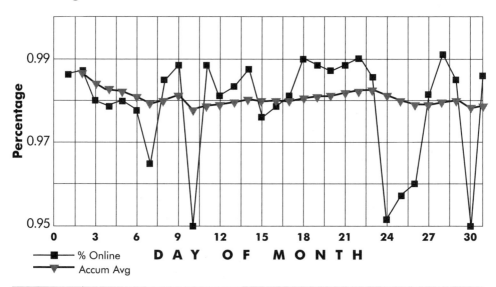

But the only way I'm going to really get down to the 189 is if I keep up the regime of exercise and watching those calories; if I do it every day, day-in, day-out, until I've given my body enough time to get down to my goal. The reality is that a pound consists of 3,500

calories and if I can somehow take off 3,500 calories in a week I can take off a pound. If I can take off enough weight a week I can reach my goal. Let's say I do want to take off the 20 pounds or so I need to take off to get down to 189. I know what I have to do, and I know it's going to take some effort and some time.

If I'm serious about it, and as long as there aren't other mitigating circumstances over which I have no control that make the original goal impossible, then there is no reason I can't actually make my goal.

If I have a scorecard that gives the proper celebratory "bounce" to each pound I manage to lose, that will help make the difference.

Percentage of time on-line

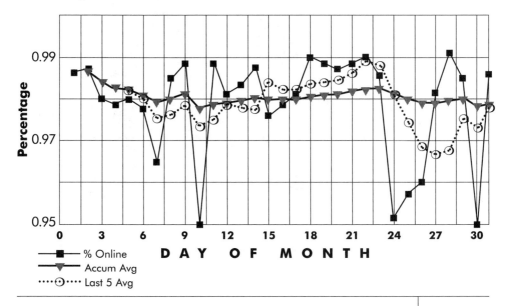

Make It Yours!

By taking care to measure that which is significant, we put ourselves into position to realize significant results. Put bounce in your scorecards by making sure they are designed to represent what is relevant and what is readable; and don't be afraid to tinker with them when they don't. Don't be a Wrigley Field, mired in tradition at the expense of sound communication. Part of the synergy of scorekeeping is that the more effectively we keep score, the more we can see how to improve our scorekeeping.

Create Your Own Scorecards

24

CHICKEN FOOT

All coaches coach players;
great coaches coach coaches.

Common Sense Coaching

We've talked extensively about the importance of the score-coard enabling a coach and player to agree on when, what kind, and how much feedback is appropriate. Now, as we concentrate on constructing scorecards, let's look at an effective construction method that allows us to more easily visualize exactly what our various roles are, no matter where we might happen to sit in the company hierarchy.

Why do we want to know our roles? Because then we know what to keep score on. When we know what to keep score on, we know how we can win.

I call this the chicken-foot diagram, an illustration of which can be found in this chapter. Look at it carefully, because whatever your business, it can easily be applied to your particular scorekeeping needs.

To illustrate the chicken-foot, let's turn to a professional sports franchise. We'll choose a franchise in the National Football League, but this is just an example. Any franchise, and any sport, will do.

The franchise begins with an owner. It's easy for the owner to identify what's necessary for him or her to come to work and win. The franchise needs to sell enough tickets, make a good enough television deal, generate enough merchandising sales, sell enough hot dogs and beverages, and so on. The franchise needs to turn a profit, in other words. That's the owner's assignment. That's what will determine success or failure.

The first thing the owner does is hire a coach.

With the coach, there's also little problem in identifying how to win. Organize a team that wins games, championships, and attracts large crowds.

So far the organization is easy. The owner and the coach both know how they can win.

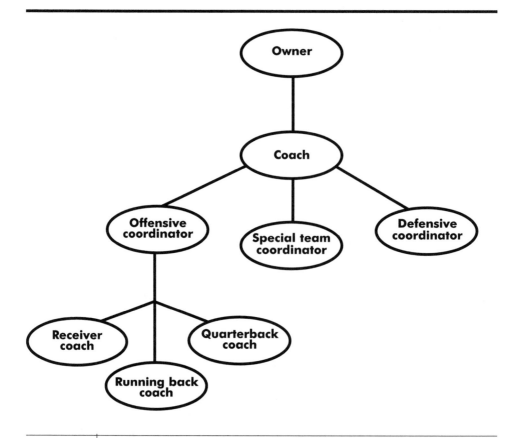

But as the coach hires more people, what does he or she tell them in regards to winning and losing? Do they assume the same accountabilities as the coach? As the owner? Of course not. The new people are hired to take care of specific areas that, when added together, will hopefully produce the organization's desired goals.

This is where the chicken foot begins to take shape.

Two of the football coach's first hires will be an offensive coordinator and a defensive coordinator, one coach each to oversee the offense and defense on the football team. When the offensive coordinator is hired, his instructions are to set up the offense. The coach might break that job description down into specific statistics—how many average yards per passing play are expected, how many average yards per running play, how many average total yards per game, how many average points per game, and so on. The idea being, if the offense reaches these averages, the winning will take care of itself.

The coach tells the same kinds of things to the new defensive coordinator, who will be expected to meet certain standards in terms of numbers of interceptions, sacks, pass deflections, fumble recoveries, and so on. Here, too, the idea is to set up defensive goals that, when met, will facilitate winning football games.

And on and on the "chicken-foot" spreads. The offensive coordinator will, in turn, hire individual coaches in charge of passing, running, line play, and so forth. Each of these coaches will have his own area to concentrate on and accept responsibility for. Same with the defense. There will be a coach for the defensive backs. He'll concentrate on interceptions and pass defense. There will be a line coach. He'll concentrate on quarterback sacks, interior blocking, and so forth.

The process repeats itself, from head coach to coordinator to quarterback coach to offensive line coach, to receivers coach, and again down another track from defensive coordinator to defensive line coach, to defensive secondary coach, to special teams coach ... until, at some point, the staff is complete and, ideally, all of the responsibilities necessary to achieve the company's overall goals—of winning and turning a profit—are accounted for.

In the example of a football franchise, it's easy to see the separation of responsibility and, hence, the separation of scorecards. It's easy to see why the scorecard for the quarterback coach, for instance, will be completely distinguishable from the scorecard for the linebacker coach. Each will measure what is pertinent to his area, limited to his particular responsibilities. The quarterback coach will set quotas and goals around pass completions, yards-per-pass, and the lack of quarterback sacks. By contrast, the linebacker coach will set quotas and goals around denied pass completions, diminishing yards-per-pass, and an abundance of quarterback sacks. And their scorecards will reflect that.

It's also easy, with this example, to see how Performance Standards and *Wow!* and *How?* zones can be easily defined and utilized. If the offensive coordinator produces an offense that goes beyond what the franchise deems as satisfactory (Performance Standards), then he's in the *Wow!* zone and the coach will be duty-bound to celebrate with him and give him an abundance of positive feedback. If the coordinator produces an offense that comes up short, however; if the scorecard reflects a productivity that falls on the other side of the Performance Standard, then it's going to be the coach's responsibility to ask *How* he might help improve the offense. And if the

Performance standards and the *How?* and *Wow!* zones can easily be defined and utilized.

offense goes so far below the Performance Standard that it moves beyond the End Line, then the offensive coordinator will be in jeopardy of being released or reassigned.

There's an obvious domino effect at play in the chicken-foot diagram. There's also an order and stability that keeps straight everyone's responsibilities and allows for a coach and player to know who is charge of what area.

Universally Applicable

The beauty of the chicken-foot system is that it can essentially be applied across the board. No matter what your business, no matter how big or small, complicated or simple, compact or spread out, when scorecards are developed with coaches and players specifically identified, as well as their duties, everyone is going to have a clear picture of what is expected and what defines success. In nearly two decades of association with a wide range of companies around the world, we have yet to find a business or organization that is not easily conformable to the simple chicken-foot diagram.

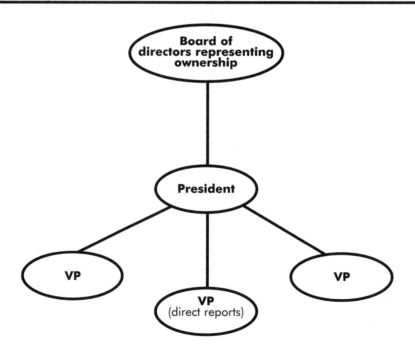

Also encouraging is experience we've had with individuals who have been able to use at least a portion of the chicken foot to better identify their duties and responsibilities. Just because you may find yourself in the employ of people who either ignore or stridently oppose the concept of scorekeeping doesn't mean you can't implement its usefulness for your own circumstances. It's a simple process of establishing who your coach is, what he or she wants, and then setting up a scorecard that helps you keep track of just how much of it you're giving.

Make It Yours!

Turf protecting is one of the most serious problems in American business. It can be eliminated by setting up a simple chicken-foot diagram that paves the way for a scorekeeping system that allows everyone involved to keep the correct score, and to accurately define responsibilities. Large or small, national or multinational, if you take care of the fundamentals of effective scorekeeping, you allow one and all to be able to every day answer the question: How do I win?

25

THE ROLEX

Common Sense Coaching

When I was just getting started in this business of "productivity improvement," there was something I wanted badly.

It wasn't my own Fortune 500 Company. It wasn't financial security for the rest of my life. It wasn't to write a best-selling book.

I wanted those things, of course, and if I'd sat down with a piece of paper back in 1974 when I was 30 years old I'm sure I would have listed those as my ambitions. But those were far-off goals, way out there on the horizon. I wanted them, although I didn't expect them immediately.

What I wanted right then was a Rolex watch.

I saw it one day when I was walking through the mall. It was in a jewelry case, sitting like a crown jewel in the middle of the display window. A Rolex President.

I'll leave it to the psychologists as to just why I coveted that watch, but I did. I wanted it. Wanted it badly.

It made no sense. I could have gotten a quartz watch for thirty dollars that kept perfectly good time, but it was that Rolex President I wanted. I had recently affiliated with a group of successful businessmen in Texas and they all had Rolexes. I suppose that had something to do with it. They called them "Texas Timexes."

The Texas Timex I had my eye on was 18-karat gold and in 1975 it had a retail selling price of $3,000.

Well, I didn't have $3,000. I didn't have anything close to $3,000. I had recently started my own business, gone through an expensive divorce settlement, and was living in a 600-square-foot apartment with a new bride. Three thousand dollars, as a matter of fact, was exactly the amount of money my wife had spent on her brand new Datsun B210 sedan just prior to meeting me.

When I walked into the jewelry store and asked the salesman if I could look at the Rolex, he naturally wanted to make a sale.

The salesman was an acquaintance of mine who knew I was starting out in my own business—the business of selling success—and he already regarded me as a successful local businessman. Looks can be deceiving. He told me if I gave them a thousand dollars down then they'd finance the balance. He didn't know I didn't have a thousand dollars. I thanked him for his time and left the store.

Two weeks later I was back. I asked if I could try that watch on again.

This time the salesman had a different approach. He told me about a pool table he'd bought recently, even though he couldn't afford the full price all at once. He'd put the pool table on lay-away, meaning the store kept it until he'd paid for most of it, then they let him take it home. He said if I'd give him $500 they'd consider the Rolex on lay-away, and after I paid another $500 I could take it home.

The salesman didn't know I didn't have $500, either. I again thanked him for his time and left the store.

Two weeks later, I was back again.

Business was starting to pick up. I'd just made a sale. But the only money I had on me was five dollars.

As I again tried the watch on and the salesman renewed his pitch about the lay-away program, I cut him off and said, "But I feel like I need to earn it. Tell you what, I'll come down here every fourth Saturday and I'll pay five dollars for every person I'm able to enroll in my new program. When I pay it off completely, I'll own it, and I'll take it home."

Then, as the salesman was mulling this over, I added, "I want to know if you have any confidence in me."

"What do you mean?" he asked.

"I'll give you all the money I have on me to start the contract," I answered.

"Well how much do you have on you?"

"Not until you agree to the deal," I persisted. "I'm good for it," I continued. I could see he was hesitating. "You keep the watch. You can't lose. You can have all the money I have. You can search me if you want to. I'll give you every cent I have on me. Just tell me if we have a deal."

The salesman said to hang on a minute, he'd go over and talk to his manager.

When he came back he tried again. "How much you got?"

"I'm not going to tell you," I said. "This is the time for you to take the leap of faith with me. What do you say? I mean, what do you have to lose?"

"All right," he finally said, "We've got a deal."

I reached in my pocket and pulled out the oldest five-dollar bill he'd ever seen in his life.

"Deal," I said, and stuck out my hand.

I thought the salesman was going to pass out.

But there was nothing he could do. A deal had indeed been struck.

From that moment on, that Rolex became an incentive for me to enroll people in the early versions of our GAME OF WORK program. The deal with myself was that I would pay five dollars toward that Rolex for every person enrolled. The more people, the closer I'd get to wearing the Rolex. Every fourth Saturday I went into the jewelry store and wrote out a check. It was usually no more than $150 and was never less than $75. Every time I made a payment they let me put the watch on my wrist and walk around the store.

Two and a half years later, I put it on my wrist and didn't take it off. That Rolex was finally paid in full.

But when did I take possession? Not the day I took it home. The day I struck the deal.

For nearly three years, long before it stayed at my house overnight, that Rolex brought me enthusiasm and helped drive my efforts.

As our business grew, I added accessories to my watch. I added a diamond dial one year, and a diamond bezel after that. But neither carried the emotional power or taught me the lessons like the original purchase.

I still have my Rolex. I remember a few years ago when we were in the Caribbean shopping in a duty-free port and I said to my wife after admiring a sparkling new watch in the jewelry case, "I think I'll trade my watch in on a new Mariner gold." She said, "You can't trade that watch in. That watch is too much a part of our company history."

She was right, of course. There is a story behind my five-dollar Rolex. It's a story about scorekeeping.

I used that wristwatch to keep score in the early days, and there was an amazing power there. I was fortunate to discover and use that power. I hope you are just as fortunate.

Chuck Coonradt

What Is THE GAME OF WORK?

THE GAME OF WORK is an action-packed seminar to provide you with the keys to enjoying work as much as play.

THE GAME OF WORK examines the phenomenon that people often work harder at sports and athletic endeavors than they do at their jobs. Why? Because in sports, a participant has constant feedback on how he or she is doing—the score is known and the effort necessary to win is established. In work, feedback is often unreliable, inconsistent, or nonexistent. The participant seldom knows the score or what it takes to win.

Chuck Coonradt is a graduate of Michigan State University and did his graduate studies at UCLA. He is an internationally recognized consultant and lecturer in the field of goal setting and profit improvement.

As author of THE GAME OF WORK, Chuck Coonradt takes the winning techniques of recreation and applies them to the workplace to increase profitability and productivity. A small sample of clients who have implemented THE GAME OF WORK include the Quaker Oats Company, Pepsi-Cola Company, Dow Chemical, Fleming Companies Inc., General Foods Corporation, United Artists Cablesystem Corporation, Young Electric Sign Company, Martin Door Manufacturing, Wendy's, xpedex/International Paper, Columbia HCN, Hoechst Celanese, and Browning-Ferris Industries.

What You Can Expect to Learn

- *A fresh look at motivation and scorekeeping through*: attitudes of winners—choices—observation—judgments—scorekeeping—implementing a system—turning measurement into a benefit—setting criteria for goals
- *Motivation*: self-evaluation—feedback—types of motivation—coaching
- *Feedback*: graphs and charts—rules and mechanics of scorecards—guidelines for effective feedback
- *Areas of control*: the power of the Results to Resources Ratio as a scorekeeping tool
- *How to set up a Results to Resources scorekeeping system*
- *Goal setting and motivation*
- *Personal goal-setting*
- *Understanding the field of play*
- *Learning how to win every day!*

Professional Services

- Speeches (two-hour, four-hour, or full-day)
- Workshops for your personnel, customers, associations, company meetings
- Implementation—a fully customized program of six half-days of specific *GAME OF WORK* implementation with *guaranteed results*
- Ski & Scheme—three-day executive ski retreat at Deer Valley Resort

For additional information, call:

1-800-438-6074
or write:
THE GAME OF WORK
1912 Sidewinder Drive, Suite 201
Park City, Utah 84060
Fax: (435) 649-2928
email: game@gameofwork.com
www.gameofwork.com

INDEX